delicious. MAGAZINE

EASY CHICKEN

Edited by Debbie Major

Ma   Editor

Matthew Drennan

HarperCollins*Publishers*

MAGAZINE

delicious.

EASY CHICKEN

HarperCollins*Publishers*
77–85 Fulham Palace Road,
Hammersmith, London W6 8JB
www.harpercollins.co.uk

First published by HarperCollins*Publishers* 2009

10 9 8 7 6 5 4 3 2 1

© Seven Publishing Group Ltd 2009

A catalogue record of this book is available from the British Library

ISBN-13   978-0-00-729254-7

Printed and bound in China by South China Printing Co.

contents

introduction

At **delicious.** magazine, we receive many letters and emails from readers requesting recipes, but if there's one ingredient that proves more popular than any other it's chicken. It's easy to cook, quick to prepare and this indispensable and valuable ingredient has been a staple of British cooking for many years. Of course, chicken's popularity has meant that there is a vast choice at the supermarket or butcher, but here at **delicious.** HQ we like to opt for a good-quality, free-range bird – whether it's organic or corn-fed is up to you.

Every month, the **delicious.** food team look for new ways to cook with chicken, and inspiration comes in many forms – from restaurants we've eaten in and countries we have visited to seasonal ingredients. Here we have chosen some of the best recipes from the magazine and compiled them under chapter headings to suit your busy life: soups, snacks and light lunches, main meal salads, hot and spicy chicken, winter warmers and oven-baked and stove-top dishes. All the recipes have been tried and tested in the **delicious.** test kitchen until we are satisfied that they will read, cook and taste utterly delicious.

Matthew Drennan
delicious. Magazine Editor

Conversion tables

All the recipes in this book list only metric measurements (also used by Australian cooks). The conversions listed here are approximate for imperial measurements (also used by American cooks).

Oven temperatures

°C	Fan°C	°F	Gas	Description
110	90	225	¼	Very cool
120	100	250	½	Very cool
140	120	275	1	Cool
150	130	300	2	Cool
160	140	325	3	Warm
180	160	350	4	Moderate
190	170	375	5	Moderately hot
200	180	400	6	Fairly hot
220	200	425	7	Hot
230	210	450	8	Very hot
240	220	475	9	Very hot

Weights for dry ingredients

Metric	Imperial	Metric	Imperial
7g	¼oz	425g	15oz
15g	½oz	450g	1lb
20g	¾oz	500g	1lb 2oz
25g	1oz	550g	1¼lb
40g	1½oz	600g	1lb 5oz
50g	2oz	650g	1lb 7oz
60g	2½oz	675g	1½lb
75g	3oz	700g	1lb 9oz
100g	3½oz	750g	1lb 11oz
125g	4oz	800g	1¾lb
140g	4½oz	900g	2lb
150g	5oz	1kg	2¼lb
165g	5½oz	1.1kg	2½lb
175g	6oz	1.25kg	2¾lb
200g	7oz	1.35kg	3lb
225g	8oz	1.5kg	3lb 6oz
250g	9oz	1.8kg	4lb
275g	10oz	2kg	4½lb
300g	11oz	2.25kg	5lb
350g	12oz	2.5kg	5½lb
375g	13oz	2.75kg	6lb
400g	14oz	3kg	6¾lb

Liquid measures

Metric	Imperial	Aus	US
25ml	1fl oz		
50ml	2fl oz	¼ cup	¼ cup
75ml	3fl oz		
100ml	3½fl oz		
120ml	4fl oz	½ cup	½ cup
150ml	5fl oz		
175ml	6 fl oz	¾ cup	¾ cup
200ml	7fl oz		
250ml	8fl oz	1 cup	1 cup
300ml	10fl oz/½ pint	½ pint	1¼ cups
360ml	12fl oz		
400ml	14fl oz		
450ml	15fl oz	2 cups	2 cups/1 pint
600ml	1 pint	1 pint	2½ cups
750ml	1¼ pints		
900ml	1½ pints		
1 litre	1¾ pints	1¾ pints	1 quart
1.2 litres	2 pints		
1.4 litres	2½ pints		
1.5 litres	2¾ pints		
1.7 litres	3 pints		
2 litres	3½ pints		
3 litres	5¼ pints		

UK–Australian tablespoon conversions

1 x UK or Australian teaspoon is 5ml

1 x UK tablespoon is 3 teaspoons/15ml

1 Australian tablespoon is 4 teaspoons/20ml

soups, snacks and light lunches

Noodle, chicken and aubergine coconut laksa

Thai red curry paste and lemongrass capture the flavour of Malaysia in this popular and easy Southeast Asian dish.

SERVES 4
READY IN ABOUT 40 MINUTES

- ½ x 250g pack dried medium rice noodles (see tip below)
- 1 medium aubergine, halved lengthways and cut into 5mm slices
- 2 tbsp olive oil
- 2 tbsp Thai red curry paste
- 400ml can reduced-fat coconut milk
- 600ml chicken stock, hot
- 4 small skinless free-range chicken breasts
- 1 lemongrass stalk, bruised
- 150g sugar snap peas, halved lengthways
- ½ tsp soft light brown sugar
- Grated zest and juice of 1 lime, plus extra lime wedges to serve
- Good handful of fresh basil leaves

1. Put the noodles into a wide bowl and cover with boiling water. Set aside for 5 minutes to soften. Drain, refresh in cold water and set aside.

2. Brush the aubergine slices on both sides with oil, season with salt and put onto a baking sheet. Grill for 4–5 minutes on each side, until golden. Drain on kitchen paper.

3. Stir-fry the curry paste in a large pan or wok over a medium heat for 1 minute. Stir in the coconut milk and stock, and bring to a simmer. Add the chicken and lemongrass, cover and simmer for 10–12 minutes or until the chicken is cooked. Lift out the chicken with a slotted spoon and shred.

4. Return the chicken to the pan with the sugar snaps and aubergine slices. Simmer for 2 minutes, then stir in the noodles, sugar, lime zest and juice, and most of the basil. Heat through, season and ladle into bowls. Garnish with lime wedges and the remaining basil leaves.

★ DELICIOUS. TIP If you can't find dried medium rice noodles, use ready-to-stir-fry rice noodles and add directly to the laksa in step 3.

Variation In Malaysia, laksa is made just as often with prawns as with chicken, so replace the chicken with 300g of raw peeled prawns and add them in step 4.

Spiced chicken noodle soup

This light and spicy soup, packed with noodles, is just perfect for a filling yet healthy lunch.

SERVES 2
READY IN 20 MINUTES

2 free-range chicken breasts, bone in
4 black peppercorns
2 bay leaves
1 leek, washed and sliced
2 small carrots, halved lengthways
2 small celery sticks, halved
1 small bunch of fresh thyme
1 tsp celery salt
6 thin slices fresh root ginger
1 large medium-hot red chilli, halved lengthways
1 star anise
1 bunch of spring onions, chopped
1 large carrot, cut into matchsticks
2 blocks fine dried egg noodles
225g bag baby spinach leaves
4 tbsp soy sauce
Chilli oil, to serve (optional)

1. Put the chicken breasts into a saucepan with the next seven ingredients and 1.5 litres water. Cover, bring to the boil and simmer for 20 minutes until the chicken is cooked. Leave to cool, then lift out the chicken and remove and shred the meat, discarding the skin and bones.

2. Strain the stock into a clean saucepan and boil, if necessary, until reduced to 1 litre. Add the ginger, chilli, star anise and spring onions, and simmer for 10 minutes. Add the chicken and carrot, and simmer for 5 minutes.

3. Meanwhile, place the noodles in a large bowl, pour over boiling water to cover and leave to soak for 3–4 minutes until tender. Drain and divide between two deep serving bowls. Pile a good handful of spinach leaves on top of each.

4. Ladle the chicken, broth and vegetables over the noodles and spinach (it will wilt immediately) and serve drizzled with soy sauce, and chilli oil, if you wish.

Chicken curry puffs

These are like extremely flaky samosas. You could make your own pastry, but for those in a rush, look for a good, ready-made, all-butter puff pastry.

MAKES ABOUT **8** PUFFS
TAKES **45** MINUTES, **10–15** MINUTES
TO BAKE, PLUS COOLING

2 medium potatoes, cut
  into about 1cm dice
3 garlic cloves
2 shallots
3–4 fresh coriander sprigs,
  leaves and stems
2 tbsp mild curry powder
1 tbsp sugar, plus extra to taste
1 tsp tomato ketchup
3 tbsp soy sauce, plus extra
  to taste
3 tbsp groundnut oil
250g coarsely minced
  free-range chicken
500g block fresh puff pastry,
  cold
1 egg

1. Cook the potatoes in boiling salted water until just tender. Drain and cool. Whiz the garlic, shallots and coriander in a food processor to a near paste, then season to taste with curry powder, sugar, ketchup and soy sauce.

2. Heat the oil in a frying pan, and gently fry the curry paste for 10–15 minutes. Add the chicken and 2 tablespoons of water and fry until cooked through. Fold in the potatoes and some extra soy sauce and sugar to taste. Cool.

3. Preheat the oven to 200°C/fan 180°C/gas 6. Roll out the pastry and cut out 8 x 13cm discs. Beat the egg with 3 tablespoons of water, brush around the edges of the discs and spoon the filling into the centre. Fold into turnovers, crimp the edges, then brush with more egg.

4. Place, slightly spaced apart, on a baking sheet lined with non-stick baking paper and bake for 10–15 minutes until golden. Allow to rest for about 5 minutes before eating. Serve with yogurt and lime pickle.

Variation You can make these puffs with minced turkey instead of chicken, and to boost your 5-a-day, add a few cooked peas to the filling.

Chicken and chorizo wraps

Try a taste of Spain with these tortilla wraps filled with
paprika-flavoured chicken and a red pepper and chorizo sauce.

SERVES 4
TAKES 25 MINUTES, PLUS
30 MINUTES–3 HOURS MARINATING

2 large skinless boneless
  free-range chicken breasts
½ tsp smoked paprika
1 garlic clove, crushed
Grated zest and juice of 1 lemon
1 tbsp olive oil
Warmed tortilla wraps, to serve
142ml pot soured cream, to
  serve
Mixed dressed salad, to serve

For the sauce:
280g jar roasted red peppers
  in oil
1 small onion, thinly sliced
75g piece chorizo, skinned and
  diced

1. Cut the chicken into large chunks and put them
in a non-metallic bowl with the paprika, garlic,
lemon zest and juice and oil. Season, toss together
and marinate for at least 30 minutes or up to
3 hours.

2. Meanwhile, make the sauce. Drain and roughly
chop the peppers, reserving 2 tablespoons of the
oil. Heat the reserved oil in a large frying pan
over a medium heat. Add the onion and cook for
5 minutes until softened. Add the peppers, chorizo
and a splash of water. Cover and simmer over a
gentle heat for 5 minutes, until the sauce is
thickened. Season to taste. Cover and keep warm.

3. Preheat the grill to Medium–High. Thread the
chicken on to metal or wooden skewers (if using
wooden skewers, soak them first in water for
30 minutes to prevent scorching). Grill for about
5 minutes each side, until the chicken is
cooked through.

4. Remove the chicken from the skewers and serve
on the wraps with the sauce, soured cream and a
mixed dressed salad.

Variation For veggies, replace the chorizo
with 1 diced courgette, and use 400g of
diced halloumi instead of the chicken.

Chicken bruschetta with chilli, coriander and lemon butter

This Italian-inspired recipe makes finger licking at a barbecue quite acceptable.

SERVES 4
TAKES 20 MINUTES, 15 MINUTES ON THE BARBECUE, PLUS CHILLING

Vegetable oil, for brushing
4 boneless free-range chicken breasts, skin on
1 ciabatta loaf, cut in half, then sliced lengthways to make 4 pieces
1 large garlic clove
Crisp iceberg lettuce leaves, tomato and cucumber slices, to serve

For the chilli, coriander and lemon butter:
Good pinch of dried chilli flakes
Handful of fresh coriander, chopped
Zest and juice of 1 small lemon
225g butter, softened

1. First make the butter. Stir the chilli flakes, coriander, lemon zest and juice into the softened butter. Spoon the butter on to a large sheet of non-stick baking paper, roll up into a log shape and twist and secure the ends like a Christmas cracker. Chill until firm.

2. Meanwhile, brush the cooking grate with vegetable oil. Light the barbecue, following the manufacturer's instructions. Barbecue the chicken breasts directly over a medium heat for 10–12 minutes, turning once, until cooked through. Push the chicken to one side, to keep hot. Quickly toast and char the cut side of the ciabatta on the cooking grate, then rub the toasted side of each piece with the garlic clove. Place one piece each on four plates, toasted side up.

3. Arrange a lettuce leaf and a few tomato and cucumber slices on each piece of ciabatta. Halve the chicken breasts lengthways and arrange both slices on top. Cut the butter log into thick slices and put a slice on top of the hot chicken.

★ DELICIOUS. TIP If it's a warm day, pop the butter slices into a bowl of cold water with a few ice cubes to prevent them melting.

Variation Flavoured butters are fantastic with grilled meats. Try garlic, lemon and thyme, or pesto, or shallot, mustard and black pepper for a change.

Spicy crumbed chicken with coleslaw

This recipe beats fried chicken hands down, and it's much healthier too.

SERVES 4

TAKES 20 MINUTES, PLUS 25 MINUTES IN THE OVEN

30g packet fajita seasoning
2 tbsp plain flour
100g fresh white breadcrumbs
2 eggs
8 skinless free-range chicken drumsticks
3 tbsp vegetable oil

For the coleslaw:
4 tbsp light mayonnaise
Juice of ½ lemon
350g white cabbage, finely shredded
1 small red onion, finely sliced
1 medium carrot, coarsely grated

1. Preheat the oven to 200°C/fan 180°C/gas 6. Line a roasting tin with foil. Divide the fajita seasoning between two bowls, add the flour to one and the breadcrumbs to the other. Stir to mix. Beat the eggs in a third bowl.

2. Toss the chicken in the flour. Dip each drumstick in the egg, then evenly coat in the breadcrumbs. Add to the roasting tin, drizzle with the oil and bake for 25 minutes, turning halfway, until cooked, deep golden and crispy.

3. Meanwhile, make the coleslaw by mixing all the ingredients together in a bowl. Season and serve with the chicken.

Herby chicken and lemon rice

This satisfying dish of rice, beans, poached chicken and pancetta makes a great hearty lunch.

SERVES 4
READY IN 25 MINUTES

2 tbsp olive oil
1 large onion, finely chopped
125g cubed smoked pancetta
Leaves of 1 small fresh
  rosemary sprig, finely chopped
2 garlic cloves, finely sliced
300g mixed basmati and
  wild rice
1 litre fresh chicken stock
Approx. 500g cooked shredded
  free-range chicken
410g can cannellini beans,
  drained and rinsed
Grated zest and juice of ½ lemon
1 large bunch of fresh flatleaf
  parsley, chopped
25g freshly grated Parmesan,
  to serve

1. Heat the olive oil in a large saucepan, add the onion and cook for 5–6 minutes, until they begin to soften. Stir in the pancetta and cook for 5 minutes, until golden. Stir in the rosemary and garlic and cook for 1 minute.

2. Add the rice to the pan and stir to coat in the juices. Add the chicken stock to the pan and bring to the boil. Simmer for 15 minutes until the rice has absorbed nearly all the liquid. Add the chicken and beans, and heat for a further 5 minutes, until the rice is cooked.

3. Fork through the lemon zest, lemon juice and parsley, and season with a little salt and plenty of black pepper. Remove from the heat and spoon into warmed serving bowls or plates. Serve with the grated Parmesan for everyone to sprinkle over.

Chicken and lemon spaghetti carbonara

This quick and easy pasta dish makes a lovely change from the usual egg and bacon version.

SERVES 4
READY IN 25 MINUTES

2 tbsp extra-virgin olive oil

2 boneless free-range chicken breasts, skin on

450g dried spaghetti

175g piece smoked pancetta, cut into lardons

4 fresh sage leaves, chopped

2 large eggs, plus 2 large egg yolks

100ml double cream

Finely grated zest of 1 lemon

100g aged Grana Padano or Parmesan, finely grated

50g butter

1. Bring a pan of well-salted water to the boil. Heat half the oil in a small frying pan over a medium heat. Season the chicken and add to the pan (skin-side down). Cook for 6 minutes on each side until cooked through. Transfer to a plate and cool slightly.

2. Cook the spaghetti in the boiling water for 12 minutes or until al dente. Meanwhile, remove the skin from the chicken and shred the meat. Put the remaining oil into the frying pan over a medium–high heat, add the pancetta and cook for 3–4 minutes, until golden. Stir in the sage and remove from the heat.

3. Mix the eggs, yolks, cream and lemon zest together in a bowl. Drain the spaghetti, tip back into the pan and add the pancetta, chicken, egg and cream mixture, two-thirds of the cheese, the butter and some freshly ground black pepper. Toss together well, but do not return to the heat. The residual heat from the spaghetti will be sufficient to cook the eggs but still keep them smooth and creamy. Serve sprinkled with the remaining cheese.

Fruity chicken, apple and cheese pies

These small, palm-sized savoury pies are ideal for lunchboxes and picnics.

MAKES 9
TAKES 30 MINUTES, 25–30 MINUTES
COOKING, PLUS CHILLING AND COOLING

350g plain flour
175g lightly salted butter
175g rindless smoked back
  bacon rashers, diced
2 skinless free-range chicken
  breasts, about 350g, diced
100g mature Cheddar, finely
  diced
6 tbsp stewed apple compote
Leaves from 2 fresh
  thyme sprigs
1 medium egg, beaten
1 tsp rock salt

1. Put the flour and butter in a food processor and whiz to fine breadcrumbs. Add 5–6 tablespoons of cold water until the mixture comes together. Chill the pastry for 15 minutes.

2. Preheat the oven to 200°C/fan 180°C/gas 6. Roll out two-thirds of the pastry on a lightly floured surface. Cut out 9 discs that are 11cm diameter and use to line 9 holes of a muffin tin. Roll out the remaining pastry and cut out 9 discs that are 8cm diameter.

3. Fry the bacon and chicken in a pan for 8 minutes until cooked. Cool slightly, then mix in the cheese, apple compote, the leaves from 1 thyme sprig and some seasoning. Divide the mixture among the pastry cases, packing it in firmly. Brush a little water around the pastry rim. Put the remaining pastry circles on top, press the edges together to seal, and then roll any overlapping pastry back to cover the rims. Brush with egg, scatter with the remaining thyme and rock salt, and bake for 25–30 minutes until golden. Cool in the tin for 10 minutes then transfer to a wire rack to go cold.

Pastry-wrapped chicken and rice kedgeree

This simple pie is ideal to have in the freezer, ready to bake on those days when you don't feel like cooking.

SERVES 6

TAKES 45 MINUTES, FREEZE FOR UP TO 1 MONTH, THEN DEFROST FOR 24 HOURS, PLUS 40 MINUTES COOKING

100g long grain rice

600ml fresh chicken stock

3 skinless boneless free-range chicken breasts

75g butter

1 bunch of spring onions, finely chopped

150g chestnut mushrooms, chopped

Handful of chopped fresh flatleaf parsley

2 hard-boiled eggs, roughly chopped

Grated zest of 1 small lemon

500g pack fresh puff pastry

1 egg yolk, beaten with a little water

1. Cook the rice according to the packet instructions, drain and set aside. Meanwhile, put the stock into a pan, bring to a simmer, add the chicken and poach for 15–20 minutes, until just cooked through. Drain, cool and cut into bite-sized pieces.

2. Melt the butter in a saucepan. Add the onions and mushrooms, and cook for 2–3 minutes, until just softened. Take off the heat and mix in the rice, chicken, parsley, eggs and lemon zest.

3. Roll out the pastry to 30cm x 35cm and put it on a non-stick baking sheet. Spoon the chicken and rice mix on to one half, leaving a border at the edge. Brush the edges with water. Fold the pastry over and seal the edges.

4. Open-freeze for 4 hours on the baking sheet. Remove from the sheet, wrap in cling film and freeze again.

5. Thaw in the fridge overnight. Put a baking sheet in the oven and preheat to 200°C/fan 180°C/gas 6. Brush the pastry with the egg yolk, sprinkle with black pepper and sea salt, place on the hot sheet and bake for 40 minutes until golden.

★ DELICIOUS. TIP To bake from fresh, make up to step 3, brush with the yolk and put on to a cold baking sheet. Bake for 30 minutes.

Chicken noodle soup with mint and lemon

Adding lemon and mint to this classic noodle soup is believed to be a Portuguese innovation. And it's wonderful.

SERVES 4
READY IN 50 MINUTES

2 free-range chicken breasts, bone in if possible
2 bay leaves
1 garlic clove
4 tbsp soy sauce
2 tbsp Chinese rice wine or dry sherry
1 tsp runny honey
Juice of ½ lemon
300g straight-to-wok udon noodles
Fresh mint leaves, to garnish
Lemon slices, to garnish

1. Place the chicken, bay leaves and garlic in a pan with 1 litre of cold water. Bring to a simmer and cook for 30 minutes, until cooked through, skimming any froth from the surface. Remove the chicken and set aside.

2. Continue to simmer the broth, adding the soy sauce, rice wine or sherry, honey and lemon juice. Season, adding more soy sauce or lemon juice, if you like.

3. Blanch the noodles for 3 minutes in boiling water. Drain and divide among warmed bowls. Thinly slice the chicken and put it on top of the noodles. Pour over the broth, scatter with mint and top with a slice of lemon.

Variation If you have trouble finding udon noodles, any other type of noodle will be fine – just cook them first.

Chicken and mushrooms on bruschetta

The combination of chicken, mushrooms, thyme and lemon works beautifully in this light lunchtime dish.

SERVES 4
READY IN 25 MINUTES

2 free-range chicken breasts
1 tbsp olive oil
Leaves from 2 fresh
  thyme sprigs
50g pine nuts
8 medium button mushrooms
Juice of ½ lemon
Extra-virgin olive oil, for
  drizzling
4 slices bruschetta (see tip
  below)
2 generous handfuls of mixed
  lettuce leaves, washed and
  dried

1. Preheat the oven to its highest setting. Rub the chicken with the oil, thyme, and ½ teaspoon each of salt and cracked black pepper. Place in a small roasting tin and cook for 15 minutes, or until cooked through and golden. Set aside to cool a bit.

2. Meanwhile, place the pine nuts on a baking sheet and roast for 2–3 minutes, until golden brown. Set aside.

3. Very thinly slice the mushrooms, lay them on a plate and squeeze over the lemon juice. Drizzle with a little olive oil.

4. Prepare the bruschetta (see tip below) and put each slice on a plate. Slice the chicken very thinly and toss with the mushrooms, lettuce, any chicken juices and some seasoning.

5. Divide the salad among the slices of bruschetta and scatter with the pine nuts. Drizzle with a little more oil.

★ DELICIOUS. TIP To make bruschetta, grill or griddle good bread on both sides, rub with the cut side of a garlic clove, anoint liberally with extra-virgin olive oil and season with salt.

Spicy chicken with couscous

A sweet and spicy mixture of curry paste, mango chutney and turmeric is a great way to liven up chicken breast fillets.

SERVES 4
READY IN 25 MINUTES

1 tbsp medium–hot curry paste
1 tbsp mango chutney
½ tsp turmeric
50ml olive oil
2 x 375g packets free-range mini chicken breast fillets
300g couscous
350ml boiling vegetable stock
Good knob of butter
Handful of fresh coriander, chopped
Natural yogurt and pinch of paprika, to serve

1. Put the curry paste, chutney, turmeric and olive oil into a large bowl. Mix well. Cut the chicken fillets in half and stir into the paste until well coated. Set aside for 10 minutes.

2. Line your grill pan with foil and lay the chicken pieces on top, making sure there is space between them. Grill for 10–12 minutes, turning once, until golden and lightly charred.

3. Meanwhile, make the couscous according to the packet instructions, but using the boiling stock instead of water. When the couscous has soaked up all the liquid, run a fork through it to fluff up. Stir in the butter and coriander, and season well. Divide among four bowls, top with the chicken and serve with a good dollop of yogurt and a pinch of paprika.

Chicken and smoked mozzarella quesadillas

These hot tortilla sandwiches make a nice alternative to the usual lunchtime fare.

SERVES 4
READY IN 20 MINUTES

2 ready-to-eat cooked free-range chicken breasts, finely diced

½ small red pepper, seeded and finely diced

4 spring onions, trimmed and finely chopped

200g smoked mozzarella, finely diced

Few fresh sage leaves, finely chopped

8 soft flour tortillas

Olive oil, to grease

Watercress and cherry tomatoes on the vine, to serve

1. Put the chicken, red pepper, spring onions, mozzarella and sage into a bowl. Season and mix together.

2. Lay one tortilla flat on a board. Scatter a quarter of the chicken mixture over it, top with another tortilla and press together. Make three more quesadillas in the same way.

3. Grease 2 large frying pans with a little olive oil and put over a medium heat. Put one quesadilla into each pan and cook for 2 minutes, until golden. Invert on to a plate, then slide back into the pan and cook for another 2 minutes, until the filling is hot and the cheese just melting. Set aside while you cook the other two. Cut each quesadilla into four and serve with watercress and cherry tomatoes.

★ DELICIOUS. TIP Smoked mozzarella has a wonderful, almost nutty, flavour. If you can't find it in Italian delis, use regular mozzarella instead.

main meal
salads

Coronation chicken salad

This is a quick and easy version of the classic chicken salad recipe, except this tasty version is a little lower in calories.

SERVES 2
READY IN 10 MINUTES

150g pot natural yogurt
4 tbsp chunky mango
  chutney
75g mixed herb salad leaves
200g pack free-range roast
  chicken tikka mini fillets
125g green seedless grapes
25g toasted flaked almonds

1. In a small bowl, season the yogurt with a little salt and pepper and then swirl in the mango chutney so that they are roughly mixed together. Spoon into small pots and set aside.

2. Divide the salad leaves and arrange the tikka mini fillets on top. Scatter over the grapes, halving any large ones, followed by the toasted flaked almonds. Serve with the pots of yogurt and mango chutney dressing on the side so that you can add as little or as much as you would like.

★ DELICIOUS. TIP Try to choose a bag of mixed salad leaves that contains fresh coriander sprigs as the flavour goes very well with the spicy chicken and mango chutney.

Lemon, olive and rosemary chicken with butter bean salad

There is a Mediterranean flavour to this zesty chicken dish that's ideal for summer days.

SERVES 4
READY IN 40 MINUTES, PLUS
15 MINUTES MARINATING

Grated zest and juice of 1 lemon
1 tbsp chopped fresh rosemary
  leaves
3 garlic cloves, chopped
25g pitted mixed olives, chopped
1 tsp golden caster sugar
6–8 skinless boneless
  free-range chicken thighs
Vegetable oil, for greasing

For the butter bean salad:
2 x 400g cans butter beans,
  drained and rinsed
100ml chicken or vegetable
  stock, hot
250g cherry tomatoes, halved
200g French beans, steamed
  and halved
2 tsp sun-dried tomato paste
1 tsp white wine vinegar
4 tbsp fresh flatleaf parsley,
  chopped

1. In a large, non-metallic bowl, combine the lemon zest and juice, rosemary, garlic, olives and sugar. Season well and add the chicken. Toss to coat in the marinade, then set aside to marinate for 15 minutes.

2. Preheat the grill to Medium–High. Line the grill pan with foil, lightly grease with oil and add the chicken and its marinade – spread out in the pan. Grill for about 15 minutes or until cooked, turning and basting with the marinade as you go. Set aside for a few minutes, then thickly slice.

3. While the chicken is cooking, put the butter beans in a pan with the stock. Simmer gently for 5 minutes until the beans are hot, then drain. Stir in the remaining ingredients and season.

4. Divide the butter bean salad among four bowls, top with chicken slices and serve.

Variation To ring the changes, use any type of beans that you like for this salad – canned cannellini, flageolet, red kidney and borlotti beans, or fresh broad beans.

Spiced almond and sultana marinated chicken

This simple yet sublime salad is perfect for away-day occasions. Or just stay at home and enjoy it in the garden.

SERVES 4–6
TAKES 25 MINUTES, 2–12 HOURS MAR-INATING, PLUS CHILLING

2 tsp cumin seeds
1 garlic clove, crushed
1 medium–hot red chilli, seeded and finely chopped, plus extra-thin chilli slices, to garnish
4 tbsp olive oil
1 small bunch of fresh coriander, chopped
4 skinless free-range chicken breasts, cut into 2cm wide strips
2 tbsp toasted flaked almonds
2 tbsp sultanas
2 tbsp reduced-salt soy sauce
1 cos lettuce, torn into leaves, to serve
1 bunch of radishes, trimmed and sliced, to serve

1. Heat a large frying pan over a medium–high heat. Add the cumin seeds and shake around for about 1 minute until fragrant and toasted. Tip into a bowl and add the garlic, chilli, half the oil and half the coriander. Add the chicken and toss everything together. Cover and chill for at least 2 hours, or up to 12 hours.

2. Heat the pan over a Medium–High heat. Add the chicken and its marinade, in 2 batches, and stir-fry for 4–5 minutes until the chicken is cooked. Remove with a slotted spoon to a large bowl and mix with the almonds.

3. Reduce the heat to low and add the remaining oil and sultanas to the juices in the pan. Heat gently, remove and stir in the soy sauce and some black pepper. Pour over the chicken and almonds, mix together and cool. Stir in the remaining coriander, cover and chill until needed.

4. Arrange the lettuce leaves on a large platter and place the chicken on top. Garnish with sliced radishes and chilli.

Chicken club salad

Make this delicious, quick and easy club salad when time is really short.

SERVES 2
READY IN 10 MINUTES

2 cooked skinless free-range chicken breasts

4 cooked crispy smoked bacon rashers

80g bag mixed salad leaves

8 baby plum or Pomodorino tomatoes, halved

1 ripe avocado, peeled, stoned and sliced

6 tbsp honey and mustard vinaigrette dressing

1. Cut the chicken breasts slightly on the diagonal into thickish slices. Break the crispy smoked bacon into bite-sized pieces.

2. Tip the mixed salad leaves into a large salad bowl. Add the halved tomatoes, sliced avocado, sliced chicken and crispy bacon pieces.

3. Drizzle over the honey and mustard dressing and gently toss everything together. Serve straight away.

Garlic chicken Caesar salad

The addition of avocado adds a wonderfully rich creaminess to this classic salad.

SERVES 4
READY IN 20 MINUTES, PLUS
10 MINUTES MARINATING

4 skinless free-range chicken breasts

3 tbsp olive oil, plus extra for greasing

Finely grated zest and juice of 1 lemon

3 garlic cloves, chopped

2 tbsp fresh thyme leaves

255g bag prepared Caesar salad

1 large ripe avocado

1 small red onion, thinly sliced

1. Put the chicken breasts, one at a time, into a plastic food bag and, using a rolling pin, lightly bash out the thickest part of the chicken until it is of an even thickness. Place them in a non-metallic bowl.

2. Add the olive oil, lemon zest and juice, chopped garlic, thyme leaves and plenty of seasoning. Mix together well and leave to marinate for at least 10 minutes.

3. Preheat the grill to Medium–High. Line the grill pan with foil, lightly grease with oil and place the chicken breasts side-by-side on the foil. Grill the chicken for 12 minutes, turning halfway, until golden and cooked through.

4. Divide the bag of Caesar salad among four shallow bowls, setting aside the croutons, Parmesan and the sachet of dressing. Peel, stone and chop the avocado and scatter over the top with the sliced red onion.

5. Slice the chicken, pile on top of the salad and then scatter the croutons and Parmesan over it. Drizzle over the dressing and serve.

Variation For a vegetarian or simply lighter version of this salad, replace the chicken breasts with quartered hardboiled eggs, add a few cooked asparagus spears, then shave over some fresh Parmesan using a potato peeler.

Chargrilled chicken with roasted tomatoes, avocado, peas and mint

The chicken for this salad is chargrilled to give it a wonderful, slightly smoky flavour.

SERVES 4
TAKES 30 MINUTES, PLUS
15–30 MINUTES MARINATING

1 tsp olive oil
1½ tsp fresh lime juice
500g skinless free-range chicken breasts
200g cherry tomatoes on the vine
100g frozen or freshly shelled peas
4 Little Gem lettuce hearts, leaves separated
30g wild rocket
Handful of fresh mint leaves
4 spring onions, very thinly sliced
1 small ripe but firm avocado

For the dressing:
3 tbsp extra-virgin olive oil
1 tbsp red wine vinegar
Good pinch of caster sugar

1. Preheat the oven to 200°C/fan 180°C/gas 6. Meanwhile, whisk the oil, lime juice and some seasoning together in a shallow dish. Add the chicken, turn to coat and leave to marinate for 15–30 minutes.

2. Roast the tomatoes in the preheated oven in a non-stick roasting tin for 4–5 minutes, until the skins just burst. Remove and cut into smaller pieces. Drop the peas into a pan of salted boiling water, bring back to the boil, drain, then refresh under cold water.

3. Scatter the lettuce, rocket, mint and spring onions over 4 plates.

4. Heat a non-stick griddle or frying pan over a high heat until hot, then reduce the heat to medium. Add the chicken and cook for 6–8 minutes each side, until cooked through. Slice and place on the salad.

5. Halve, stone and peel the avocado, and slice over the salad. Scatter over the tomatoes and peas. Whisk the dressing ingredients together, season and spoon over the salad.

Shredded chicken noodle salad with ginger and peanut dressing

The combination of cold noodles and warm dressing is a surprisingly tasty contrast in this salad.

SERVES 2
READY IN 10 MINUTES

2 boneless free-range chicken breasts, preferably skin on
3 tsp grated fresh root ginger
Grated zest of 1 lime
2 tbsp groundnut or sunflower oil
2 garlic cloves, finely chopped
1 medium–hot green chilli, seeded and finely chopped
3 tbsp crunchy peanut butter
2 tsp Thai fish sauce (nam pla) or light soy sauce
2 pieces stem ginger in syrup, drained and chopped
Fresh lime juice, to taste
Brown sugar, to taste
100–120g thin or thick rice noodles
225g carrots, cut into long thin shreds
1 small green or red pepper, seeded and cut into long thin shreds
10cm piece cucumber, seeded and cut into long thin shreds
Small handful of fresh coriander leaves
2–3 tbsp roasted peanuts, roughly chopped, to garnish

1. Slash the chicken with a sharp knife. Mix together half the ginger, the lime zest and 1 tablespoon of oil, and rub it into the chicken.

2. Preheat the grill to Medium–High. Grill the chicken for 6–8 minutes on each side until cooked. Cool a little, then shred into bite-sized pieces.

3. Meanwhile, heat the remaining oil in a small pan, add the remaining ginger, the garlic and chilli, and cook very gently for 2–3 minutes. Take the pan off the heat, add the peanut butter and let it melt. Stir in 4–6 tablespoons of water, the fish or soy sauce, stem ginger, lime juice and sugar, and simmer for 2–3 minutes. Add another 2–3 tablespoons of water to make a spoonable dressing.

4. Cook the noodles according to the packet instructions. Refresh under cold water, drain well and divide between 2 bowls. Place the vegetables, most of the coriander leaves and the warm chicken on top. Spoon over the dressing and scatter with more coriander and the peanuts.

★ DELICIOUS. TIP If you have time, leave the chicken to marinate in the fridge for at least 1 hour before cooking; this will give it extra flavour.

Chicken and mango salad with a chilli lime dressing

Most supermarkets sell packets of sliced, smoked chicken breast, or look for whole smoked ones at your local deli counter.

SERVES 4
READY IN 15 MINUTES

For the dressing:
6 tbsp olive oil
Juice of 1 lime
1 red Thai (bird's eye) chilli, seeded and chopped
Small handful of fresh coriander, roughly chopped

For the salad:
2 small ripe mangoes
4 ready-to-eat chargrilled or smoked free-range chicken breasts
150g mixed salad leaves

1. Make the dressing by mixing together the oil, lime juice, chilli and coriander. Season and set aside.

2. Slice the mango flesh away from either side of the flat stones. Peel and cut the flesh into thin slices. Slice the chicken diagonally into thick strips.

3. Divide the salad leaves among four plates and top with the mango and chicken slices. Drizzle over the dressing and serve.

★ DELICIOUS. TIP The Thai bird's eye chilli in this dressing is a perfect match with the sweet mango, but if you prefer a milder taste, use larger mild red chillies and remove the seeds first.

Variation Replace the chicken with 300g of cooked and peeled large prawns. Prawns, chilli, mango and coriander are a match made in heaven.

Warm Thai chicken salad

The key to success with this salad is in the preparation, because it is important that the chicken is still warm when you serve it.

SERVES 4
READY IN 30 MINUTES

1 tbsp olive oil

450g skinless boneless free-range chicken breasts, cut into bite-sized pieces

1 small onion, very finely chopped

2 garlic cloves, crushed

2 tbsp soy sauce, plus extra to serve

2 tsp caster sugar

1–2 red Thai (bird's eye) chillies, seeded and very thinly sliced

1 cucumber

2 large carrots, cut into very thin strips

150g beansprouts

Handful each of coarsely chopped fresh mint and coriander leaves

40g roasted salted peanuts, chopped (optional)

Grated zest and juice of 1 lime, plus wedges to serve

1. Heat the olive oil in a wok or large frying pan, add the chicken and stir-fry over a high heat for 3–4 minutes. Add the onion and garlic, and stir-fry for 2 minutes. Add the soy sauce, sugar and chillies, and stir-fry for 3–4 minutes, until the chicken is browned and the sauce has reduced to a sticky glaze. Remove from the heat.

2. Cut the cucumber in half lengthways, scoop out the seeds with a teaspoon and discard. Slice the remainder on the diagonal into thin slices.

3. Add the cucumber to the chicken with the remaining ingredients and toss together to combine. Spoon on to a serving plate and serve with lime wedges to squeeze over, and soy sauce for drizzling.

Moroccan chicken and potato salad

This salad is designed to be started in the kitchen and finished on the barbecue – at the beach, countryside, wherever.

SERVES 6
READY IN 25 MINUTES

750g waxy new potatoes, washed
1 tbsp fresh lemon juice
6 tbsp extra-virgin olive oil
2 tbsp fresh mint, chopped
2 medium–hot red chillies, seeded and finely chopped
1 bunch of spring onions, chopped
1 tsp Spanish smoked paprika
2 x 238g packs free-range mini chicken breast fillets

1. Cook the potatoes in boiling salted water for 12–15 minutes until just tender. Drain well and quarter each potato. Put into a large bowl.

2. Whisk together the lemon juice, 4 tablespoons of the oil, the mint, the chillies and seasoning. Pour over the potatoes and leave them to cool. Add the spring onions and transfer to a plastic box with a lid.

3. Mix the remaining oil with the paprika. Put into another plastic box, add the chicken and mix well. Put both boxes into a cool box.

4. Light the barbecue, following the manufacturer's instructions. Barbecue the chicken for about 8–10 minutes, turning halfway, until tender. Toss the chicken with the potato salad and serve.

★ DELICIOUS. TIP You can also cook the chicken under the grill: put it on a foil-lined grill-pan and cook for 8–10 minutes, turning once, until tender.

Chicken and fennel salad with a sweet-and-sour red onion dressing

The Italian onion dressing combines beautifully in this salad with the seared chicken, fennel and watercress. Perfection.

SERVES 4
READY IN 50 MINUTES

2 large fennel bulbs, outer layer removed, then sliced lengthways

4 tbsp olive oil

3 fat garlic cloves, halved lengthways

3 fresh rosemary sprigs, halved

4 boneless free-range chicken breasts, skin on

2 x 75g bags prepared watercress, large stalks removed

For the sweet-and-sour red onion dressing:

2 tbsp olive oil

1 small red onion, chopped

4 tsp light muscovado sugar

3 tbsp red wine vinegar

2 tsp toasted sesame oil

2½ tsp dark soy sauce

1. Heat a large griddle pan over a medium heat. Brush the fennel with half the oil, season and place on the griddle with the garlic and half the rosemary. Cook for 5 minutes on each side until marked with lines. Sprinkle with 2 tablespoons of water and cook for another 3–5 minutes, until tender. Keep warm. Discard the garlic and rosemary.

2. For the dressing, heat the oil in a frying pan over a medium heat. Add the onion and cook for 5 minutes until soft and lightly browned. Add the sugar and cook for 1–2 minutes until golden. Add the vinegar, let it bubble for a few seconds, then add the sesame oil, soy sauce and some black pepper. Keep warm.

3. Season the chicken and fry, skin-side down, in the remaining olive oil with the remaining rosemary for 6–7 minutes on each side until golden. Rest for 5 minutes and then thickly slice.

4. Put the chicken, fennel and watercress into a large bowl with the dressing and toss together. Divide among four plates and serve.

★DELICIOUS. TIP If the dressing has become thick, add any chicken juices from the plate or a tablespoon of warm water to loosen it a little, before tossing it through the salad.

Vietnamese minted chicken salad

Don't skimp on the mint in this salad; it gives the dish its
unique, classic taste.

SERVES 4
READY IN ABOUT 25 MINUTES

3 small red chillies (Thai bird's
eye or medium–hot)
2 carrots, grated
Large handful of fresh
beansprouts
Large handful of fresh mint
leaves (about 30g), plus
extra leaves to garnish
2 shallots, finely sliced
3 ready-to-eat free-range
chicken breasts

For the dressing:
2 garlic cloves, crushed
2 tbsp brown sugar
1 tbsp rice vinegar
Juice of 2 limes
1 tbsp Thai fish sauce
4 tbsp vegetable oil

1. Halve, seed and thinly slice two of the chillies.
Thinly cut the remaining chilli across into thin
slices, leaving the seeds in place. Set these aside
for the garnish.

2. Put the carrots, beansprouts, mint leaves,
shallots and seeded, sliced chillies in a large bowl
and gently toss together.

3. For the dressing, put the garlic, sugar, rice
vinegar, lime juice, fish sauce, vegetable oil and
some freshly ground black pepper into a small
bowl, and whisk well.

4. Thinly slice the chicken breasts on the
diagonal. Add to the bowl with the other salad
ingredients and toss together well. Spoon on to a
serving platter.

5. Drizzle the dressing over the salad and garnish
with the extra mint leaves and chilli slices.

hot and spicy
chicken

Best-ever tandoori chicken

This barbecue recipe is one of those dishes you will want to make every summer, rain or shine.

SERVES 6

TAKES 15 MINUTES, 1–6 HOURS MARINATING, PLUS 15–18 MINUTES TO BARBECUE

4 free-range chicken legs

4 skinless boneless free-range chicken thighs

3 skinless boneless free-range chicken breasts, cut into large pieces

Juice of ½ lemon

1 tbsp paprika

6 garlic cloves, crushed

7.5cm piece fresh root ginger, sliced

3 tbsp sunflower oil, plus extra for brushing

1½ tsp cardamom seeds, finely ground

2 tbsp garam masala

250ml wholemilk natural yogurt

40g unsalted butter, melted

Mint raita, warm coriander naan bread and lemon wedges, to serve

1. Slash both sides of each leg and thigh, and put into a bowl with the breast pieces. Sprinkle with the lemon juice, paprika and some salt, and mix well. Cover and set aside for 30 minutes.

2. Put the garlic, ginger, oil, cardamom, garam masala and yogurt into a liquidiser, and blend thoroughly. Add to the chicken and mix well. Cover and chill for 1–6 hours.

3. Light the barbecue, following the manufacturer's instructions. Shake the excess marinade off the chicken and thread the breast pieces and thighs on to eight long skewers. Brush the chicken and the bars of the cooking grate with oil.

4. Cook the chicken directly over a high heat for 4 minutes each side, releasing them from the grate with a wide spatula and turning now and then until nicely marked by the grate. Remove to a plate and brush with melted butter.

5. Turn off the middle burner or push the coals to either side of the grate. Return the chicken to the grate and continue to cook over an indirect high heat for 3–5 minutes each side or until cooked through. Serve with raita, naan bread and lemon wedges.

★ DELICIOUS. TIP You can also cook the chicken in the oven, set to its highest temperature, on a rack in a roasting tin for about 20 minutes, until cooked through.

Chicken, lime and coconut parcels

These banana-leaf wrapped parcels would make an impressive dish for a special dinner party.

SERVES 4

TAKES 30 MINUTES, PLUS 2½ HOURS STEAMING

2 medium–hot green chillies, seeded
2 garlic cloves
Juice of 1 lime
1 heaped tbsp shredded dried kaffir lime leaves or grated zest of 1 lime
Handful of fresh coriander, with stalks
1 tbsp cumin seeds, dry-toasted
3 tbsp Thai fish sauce
4 tbsp coconut cream
4 banana leaves (optional, from Asian supermarkets)
4 x 250g free-range chicken legs
Medium–hot red chillies, seeded and sliced, to garnish
Steamed jasmine rice and stir-fried sugar snap peas, to serve

1. In a mini food processor, whiz the green chillies, garlic, lime juice, lime leaves or zest, coriander, cumin, fish sauce and coconut cream to a paste.

2. Cut 4 sheets of non-stick baking paper, each 30cm x 40cm (cut out 8 if you're not using banana leaves), and top each with a banana leaf, if using. Rub the paste over the chicken legs, put one on to each leaf and wrap tightly around the chicken to make a parcel. Tie each one tightly with string to seal.

3. Arrange the parcels on a raised trivet in a pan containing a little simmering water, cover with a tight-fitting lid and steam for 2½ hours, topping up the water now and then.

4. Remove the parcels from the steamer and rest for 5 minutes. Place each parcel on a plate and open it up. Garnish with the sliced chilli and serve with steamed jasmine rice and stir-fried sugar snap peas.

Variation You could use duck legs instead of chicken, and replace the green chillies with red chillies in the curry paste, if you prefer.

Thai green chicken curry

This classic soupy curry is very quick to put together and is oh-so tasty.

SERVES 4
READY IN 35 MINUTES

2 x 400ml cans coconut milk
300ml chicken stock, hot
3 fresh or dried kaffir lime leaves
5cm piece fresh root ginger,
  peeled and sliced
4 skinless free-range chicken
  breasts, cut into chunks
125g pea aubergines, or regular
  aubergines cut into 1cm dice
Handful of fresh Thai or ordinary
  basil leaves, to taste
Juice of 1 lime, to taste
1–2 tbsp Thai fish sauce (nam
  pla), to taste

For the Thai green curry paste:
1 tsp toasted cumin seeds
2 tsp toasted coriander seeds
1 tsp shrimp paste
4 garlic cloves, chopped
5cm piece fresh root ginger,
  peeled and chopped
1 tbsp soft light brown sugar
1 lemongrass stalk, outer leaves
  discarded and finely chopped
5 medium green chillies,
  seeded and chopped
1 small bunch of fresh coriander

1. For the Thai green curry paste, in a mini food processor whiz together all the ingredients into a paste with 1 teaspoon of salt.

2. Spoon the top layer of coconut cream from the cans of coconut milk into a wok or large saucepan, add the curry paste and cook over a medium heat, stirring, for 3–4 minutes.

3. Pour in the stock and remaining coconut milk. Stir in the lime leaves, ginger, chicken and aubergines, and bring to the boil. Reduce the heat and simmer gently for 15–20 minutes, until the chicken is cooked through and the sauce is slightly reduced and thickened.

4. Stir in the basil, lime juice and fish sauce, adding more, to taste. Ladle into bowls and serve with steamed jasmine rice.

★ DELICIOUS. TIP Leave the cans of coconut milk to settle for at least 24 hours before opening. The coconut cream will settle in a thick layer on the top.

Variation Thai curries are very versatile. Replace the chicken with prawns, simmering them for just 3 minutes in step 3, or use chunks of prepared butternut squash, simmered until just tender.

Moroccan chicken stew with lemon and olives

This stew is flavoured with a 'gremolata' – a beautiful citrusy mix of very finely chopped lemon zest, garlic and parsley.

SERVES 4
READY IN 45 MINUTES

2 tsp olive oil

1 small onion, finely chopped

4 garlic cloves, crushed

5cm piece fresh root ginger, finely grated

½ tsp turmeric

4 skinless free-range chicken breasts

1 small cinnamon stick

Pinch of saffron

600ml chicken stock, hot

Grated zest and juice of 1 small lemon

Handful each of fresh mint and fresh flatleaf parsley, finely chopped

275g couscous

15g pine nuts, toasted

25g small black or green olives

1. Heat the oil in a large pan. Add the onion and cook, stirring occasionally for 5 minutes, until softened. Add all but 1 teaspoon of the crushed garlic, and the ginger and turmeric, and cook for 1 minute. Add the chicken, cinnamon, saffron, stock and lemon juice. Season, bring to a simmer and cook, uncovered, for 20 minutes or until the chicken is tender.

2. Meanwhile, mix together the remaining garlic, the lemon zest, mint and parsley to make a 'gremolata'. Set aside.

3. Lift the chicken on to a plate with a slotted spoon. Cover to keep hot. Increase the heat and boil the sauce for 10 minutes or until it is well-flavoured and reduced by about half.

4. Meanwhile, put the couscous in a large bowl and pour over 450ml boiling water, cover and stand for 5 minutes. Uncover and stir through the pine nuts.

5. Return the chicken to the pan along with the olives and gremolata, and stir. Serve with the couscous.

Ginger-roasted chicken with Bengali-spiced squash

A traditional British classic with an Indian twist.

SERVES 4
READY IN ABOUT 1½ HOURS

1.5kg whole free-range
  chicken
1 tbsp finely grated fresh
  root ginger
2 tbsp olive oil
5 tbsp fresh lemon juice

For the Bengali-spiced squash:
2–3 tbsp sunflower oil
1 medium onion, cut into thin
  wedges
2 garlic cloves, finely chopped
1 medium–hot red chilli,
  seeded and finely chopped
2.5cm fresh root ginger,
  finely grated
Seeds from 8 green cardamom
  pods, lightly crushed
1 tsp sweet paprika
2 tsp ground coriander
1 tsp ground cumin
½ tsp hot chilli powder
2 x 450g kabocha or butternut
  squash, peeled, seeded and
  cut into long thin wedges

1. Preheat the oven to 220°C/fan 200°C/gas 7.
Season the chicken cavity then smear with the
grated ginger. Tie the legs together with string and
put the chicken into a large roasting tin. Rub with
olive oil and season. Roast for 20 minutes.

2. Meanwhile, heat the sunflower oil in a large
frying pan. Add the onion wedges, garlic, chilli and
ginger, and cook over a low heat for 5 minutes until
the onions are just tender. Add the spices and cook
for a few seconds. Add the squash wedges and toss
everything together well.

3. Lower the oven temperature to 200°C/fan
180°C/gas 6. Remove the chicken from the
oven and pour away the excess fat from the tin.
Sprinkle 1 tablespoon of lemon juice over the
chicken. Return to the oven and roast for another
15–20 minutes, spooning over more lemon juice
every 5 minutes.

4. Spoon the squash and onion wedges around
the chicken and return to the oven for a further
35–40 minutes until the chicken is cooked and the
squash is tender and lightly browned.

Spicy chicken nasi goreng

This Indonesian recipe is very easy and speedy to put together.

SERVES 4
READY IN 25 MINUTES

3 medium eggs

3 tbsp vegetable oil

6 shallots, finely sliced

3 tbsp medium–hot curry paste

2 skinless boneless free-range chicken breasts, sliced into strips

300g freshly cooked basmati rice

200g small cooked and peeled prawns

½ cucumber, peeled, seeded and diced

Handful of fresh coriander, roughly chopped

Prawn crackers, to serve

Kecap manis (a thick sweet Indonesian soy sauce), to serve

1. Beat the eggs and some seasoning together in a bowl. Heat 1 teaspoon of the oil in a large, deep non-stick frying pan over a medium heat. Add half the eggs in a thin layer and cook for a few minutes, until set and golden underneath. Tip out, roll up, cool, then finely slice. Add another teaspoon of the oil to the frying pan and cook the remaining eggs as before.

2. Heat the remaining oil in the pan and fry the shallots for 5 minutes, until crisp and golden. Remove with a slotted spoon and drain on kitchen paper. Discard the oil and wipe the pan clean.

3. Add the curry paste and chicken to the pan, and stir-fry for 3–4 minutes, until it is nearly cooked through. Add the rice and prawns, and stir-fry for 1 minute. Remove from the heat, add the sliced omelettes, crispy shallots, cucumber and coriander, and toss together well. Spoon into warmed bowls and serve with prawn crackers and kecap manis.

Thai chicken coconut noodles

Carrots and green beans are good fridge stand-bys, but you can make this dish more authentic by using red peppers, sugar snap peas and beansprouts instead.

SERVES 4
READY IN ABOUT 30 MINUTES

2 x 250g packets dried medium egg noodles
1 tbsp olive oil
2 tbsp Thai red curry paste
400ml can reduced-fat coconut milk
600ml chicken stock, hot
4 small skinless boneless free-range chicken breasts
1 lemongrass stalk, bruised
150g green beans, halved lengthways
2 carrots, cut into thin sticks
1 tsp soft light brown sugar
Grated zest and juice of 1 lime, plus lime wedges to serve
Good handful of fresh basil leaves

1. Put the noodles into a bowl, cover with boiling water and set aside for 5 minutes, to soften. Drain, refresh in cold water and drain again. Toss in half the oil.

2. Heat the remaining oil in a large pan over a medium heat. Add the curry paste and stir-fry for 1 minute. Add the coconut milk, stock, chicken and lemongrass, cover and simmer for 12 minutes. Using a slotted spoon, lift the chicken out on to a plate and roughly chop.

3. Return the chicken to the pan with the beans and carrots, and simmer for 2 minutes. Stir in the noodles, sugar, lime zest and juice, and most of the fresh basil leaves, and heat through.

4. Season and ladle into bowls. Garnish with lime wedges and the remaining basil leaves.

Chinese poached chicken with ginger

This Asian-style chicken is very moist, very tasty and very low in fat, too.

SERVES 4
READY IN 1½ HOURS

1.5–1.75kg whole free-range chicken
4 spring onions, sliced
5cm piece fresh root ginger, thinly sliced
Steamed basmati rice, to serve

For the table seasonings:
1 tsp Szechuan peppercorns
1 tsp black peppercorns
3cm piece fresh root ginger
1 garlic clove, chopped
3 tbsp dark soy sauce
3 tbsp rice wine vinegar
1 tsp caster sugar
1 red chilli, seeded and thinly sliced

For the salad:
1 cos lettuce heart, torn into small pieces, washed
20g fresh coriander sprigs
4 spring onions, halved and finely shredded
½ cucumber, peeled and sliced

1. Remove any fat and all the skin from the chicken. Rub inside and out with a little salt and set aside for 20 minutes.

2. Put 3.6 litres of water, the spring onions and ginger in a large pan. Bring to the boil. Add the chicken and bring back to the boil. Cover and simmer gently for 20 minutes. Then remove from the heat and set aside for 1 hour.

3. For the seasonings, heat a frying pan over a high heat. Add the peppercorns and shake for a few seconds. Remove from heat and coarsely crush them in a mortar, mix with a little salt and tip into a bowl. Finely grate the ginger and mix with the garlic and soy in a second bowl. Mix the vinegar, sugar and red chilli in a third bowl.

4. Drain the chicken and cut into pieces. Arrange on a warm serving plate.

5. Combine all the salad ingredients in a bowl. Serve with the chicken and seasonings, along with some steamed basmati rice.

Black pepper chicken (Murgh kali mirch)

Unlike many slow-cooked Indian curries, this one can be ready in next to no time.

SERVES 4
READY IN 30 MINUTES

2 tbsp vegetable oil
2 medium onions, sliced
2 medium–hot green chillies, seeded and sliced
8 fresh or dried curry leaves
1 green pepper, seeded and sliced
4 garlic cloves, sliced
2 tbsp Madras curry paste
450g skinless boneless free-range chicken pieces, cut into chunky strips
1 tsp crushed black peppercorns
Steamed basmati rice, to serve

1. Heat the oil in a large frying pan over a medium heat. Add the onions, chillies, curry leaves, green pepper and garlic, and fry for 5–6 minutes, until softened and lightly browned.

2. Stir in the curry paste and fry for 1 minute. Add the chicken and fry for 10–15 minutes until just cooked through. If the mixture looks a little dry, add a few tablespoons of water. Season to taste with salt, and then stir in the crushed black peppercorns. Serve with steamed basmati rice.

Indian spiced butter chicken (Murgh tikka makhani)

This classic tandoori-style chicken is served here with an unusual mildly spiced and creamy sauce.

SERVES 4

TAKES 45–50 MINUTES, PLUS OVERNIGHT MARINATING

8 skinless free-range chicken drumsticks
4 tbsp tandoori curry paste
1 tbsp natural yogurt

For the sauce:
4–5 green cardamom pods
2 tbsp chopped cashew nuts
8 medium tomatoes, halved
2 bay leaves
50g butter
1 tsp ground cardamom
½ tsp dried fenugreek leaves (optional)
1 tsp clear honey
75ml single cream
Garlicky spiced lentils or steamed rice, to serve

1. Make 2 deep cuts in each drumstick. Mix the curry paste with the yogurt and spread over the chicken. Leave to marinate in the fridge for a couple of hours, or overnight.

2. Preheat the oven to 190°C/fan 170°C/gas 5. Put the drumsticks into a foil-lined roasting tin and roast for 25–30 minutes or until cooked through.

3. Meanwhile, make the sauce. Gently crush the cardamom pods with the back of a teaspoon and put the seeds in a saucepan with the cashew nuts, tomatoes, bay leaves and butter. Cover and cook over a medium heat for 20 minutes. Transfer to a liquidiser or food processor and blend until smooth.

4. Return the sauce to the pan and cook over a medium heat for 5 minutes. Add the ground cardamom, fenugreek leaves, if using, honey and cream. Season to taste and simmer for a further 5 minutes.

5. Lift the chicken on to warmed serving plates and pour over the sauce. Serve with some garlicky spiced lentils or steamed rice.

Kashmiri butter chicken

This is a wonderfully simple but spectacular dish, ideal for a special occasion.

SERVES 4
READY IN 1¼ HOURS

¾ tsp cumin seeds
¾ tsp fennel seeds
¼ tsp cardamom seeds (not pods)
Large pinch of kalonji (black onion or nigella seeds)
8 black peppercorns
1cm piece cinnamon stick
2 cloves
Large pinch of grated nutmeg
8cm piece fresh root ginger
1 medium onion, finely chopped
4 garlic cloves, crushed
1 tbsp fresh lemon juice
½ tsp chilli powder (optional)
2 tsp paprika
2 tbsp sunflower oil
1.5kg whole free-range chicken, jointed into 8 pieces (see page 184)
40g butter
3 tbsp tomato purée
1 tsp salt
1 tbsp light muscovado sugar
150ml double cream
1 small bunch of fresh chopped coriander leaves, to garnish
Naan bread or basmati rice, to serve

1. Heat a small frying pan over a medium heat. Add the first 7 ingredients and shake them around for a few seconds until lightly toasted. Tip into a spice grinder and grind to a powder. Stir in the nutmeg. Grate half the ginger and finely shred the rest.

2. Put into a small food processor the onion, garlic, grated ginger, lemon juice, chilli powder (if using), paprika, together with the spice powder and 1 tablespoon of the oil, and blend to a smooth paste.

3. Heat the remaining oil in a pan, add the chicken and fry over a medium–high heat until lightly browned. Set aside on a plate.

4. Add the butter and spice paste to the pan, and fry for 3–4 minutes. Add the tomato purée, 250ml of water, the salt and the sugar. Cover and simmer for 10 minutes.

5. Stir in the shredded ginger, cream and chicken, cover and simmer for 15–20 minutes until it is cooked through. Uncover, sprinkle with coriander and serve with naan bread or basmati rice.

Mexican chicken skewers with guacamole

A simple summertime dish that's great for the barbecue.

MAKES 8
TAKES 20 MINUTES, PLUS 30 MINUTES
MARINATING

3 tbsp olive oil
1 garlic clove, crushed
1 tsp ground cumin
½ tsp cayenne pepper
3 skinless boneless free-range
  chicken breasts, cut
  into bite-sized pieces
1 small red pepper, seeded
  and cut into bite-sized pieces
1 small green pepper, seeded
  and cut into bite-sized pieces
1 small onion, cut into 8 wedges
Small pot guacamole, to serve

1. Light the barbecue, following the manufacturer's instructions. Put the oil, garlic and spices into a bowls and mix together. Add the chicken, mix well and leave to marinate at room temperature for 30 minutes.

2. Meanwhile, soak 8 bamboo or wooden skewers in cold water for the same length of time.

3. Thread the chicken, peppers and onion alternately on to the skewers. Brush any remaining marinade on to the peppers and onions. Put on an oiled cooking grate and cook directly over a medium heat for 10-12 minutes, turning halfway. Serve with the guacamole.

★DELICIOUS. TIP You could also cook these kebabs under a medium–hot grill for 10–12 minutes, turning once.

Chicken curry

A simple tomato-based curry that's packed full of flavour.

SERVES 6
READY IN 55 MINUTES

4 tbsp vegetable oil

2 onions, halved and sliced

4 garlic cloves, crushed

3cm piece fresh root ginger, grated

150g rogan josh curry paste

8 fresh or 4 dried curry leaves (optional)

12 skinless free-range chicken thigh fillets

500g potatoes, peeled and cut into large chunks

2 small aubergines, cut into large chunks

400g can chopped tomatoes

750ml hot chicken stock

200g trimmed French beans

Naan bread or steamed rice, to serve

1. Heat the oil in a large, heavy-based pan, add the onions and fry for 5 minutes. Add the garlic and ginger, and cook for 30 seconds. Stir in the curry paste and curry leaves, if using, and fry for 1 minute. Add the chicken and cook for 10 minutes, stirring occasionally.

2. Add the potatoes, aubergines, tomatoes, stock and some salt and black pepper. Cover and cook for 15 minutes. Uncover and cook for another 10 minutes until the potatoes are very tender.

3. Add the beans and cook for 3–4 minutes until they are tender. Serve with steamed rice or warm naan bread.

★ DELICIOUS. TIP Fresh curry leaves give this an authentic flavour. You can buy them in Indian stores, or get dried ones from large supermarkets.

Methi chicken with lentils and coriander

This fantastic chicken curry is flavoured with fenugreek, a spice that lends an almost smoky flavour to the lentil sauce.

SERVES 4

READY IN 1 HOUR 20 MINUTES

5 small onions, 3 cut into fine rings and 2 finely chopped

4 tbsp sunflower oil

1 long red chilli, seeded and chopped

4 garlic cloves, chopped

4cm fresh root ginger, peeled and finely sliced

½ tsp turmeric

8 skinless free-range chicken thigh fillets, each cut into 4

½ tsp each toasted fenugreek and cumin seeds, lightly crushed

150g red split lentils, soaked for 20 minutes

250g natural yogurt

Few fresh coriander leaves and roasted cashew nuts, to serve

1. Preheat the oven to 180°C/fan 160°C/gas 4. Fry the onion rings in 1 tablespoon of oil until golden, and set aside.

2. Put the chopped onions, chilli, garlic and ginger in a blender with 3 tablespoons of water and purée. Heat 1 tablespoon of oil in a frying pan, add the purée and fry over a medium heat for 10 minutes, stirring. Stir in the turmeric.

3. Season the chicken and brown it in the rest of the oil in a flameproof casserole. Add the onion purée, toasted spices, lentils and 500ml water. Cover and transfer to the oven for 40 minutes, adding a small amount of boiling water after 30 minutes if it has become a little dry. Turn off the oven.

4. Whisk the yogurt and mix it into the chicken. Return to the oven and leave for 5 minutes. Serve in bowls, scattered with the coriander leaves, onion rings and cashew nuts.

★ DELICIOUS. TIP Serve this dish with poppadums and raita.

winter
warmers

Pot-roast cider chicken with creamy onions and Little Gem lettuce

Cooking a roast chicken in this way gives it maximum moistness, so there's no need to make any gravy.

SERVES 2–3

TAKES 15 MINUTES, PLUS 1½ HOURS ROASTING

1.5kg whole free-range chicken
330ml dry cider
2 large onions, sliced
4 fresh thyme sprigs, leaves only
142ml pot double cream
4 Little Gem lettuce hearts, quartered
Mashed potatoes, to serve

1. Preheat the oven to 200°C/fan 180°C/gas 6. Put the chicken in a large casserole dish, pour over the cider and stir in the onions and thyme. Season, cover, and roast for 45 minutes.

2. Uncover the chicken and roast for a further 45 minutes, until golden on top and cooked through. Transfer the bird to a plate to rest for 5 minutes.

3. Put the casserole on the hob over a low heat and pour in the cream to warm through. Add the lettuce, cover and cook gently for 3–4 minutes, until the lettuce is tender. Season to taste.

4. Carve the chicken and serve with the lettuce, pan juices and some mashed potatoes.

Variation Replace the Little Gem lettuce with peas, if you like.

Coq au vin

A classic one-pot dish that will hit the spot on a cold winter night.

SERVES 4

TAKES ABOUT 1 HOUR, PLUS OVERNIGHT MARINATING AND COOLING

75cl bottle of good red wine

4 tbsp brandy

4 free-range chicken thighs and 4 drumsticks, skin on

12 pickling onions or small shallots, peeled

2 celery sticks, thickly sliced

2 medium carrots, thickly sliced

2 garlic cloves, bruised

2 bay leaves

Few fresh thyme sprigs, plus extra to garnish

25g plain flour, seasoned, plus 1 tbsp

1 tbsp olive oil

15g butter

2 x 70g packs diced pancetta (or use chopped streaky bacon rashers)

250g chestnut mushrooms, wiped clean and halved if large

Small handful of chopped fresh parsley, to garnish

1. Boil the red wine and brandy until reduced by a third. Cool.

2. Put the chicken into a bowl with the onions, celery, carrots, garlic, bay leaves and thyme. Pour over the wine, cover, and chill overnight.

3. The next day, preheat the oven to 180°C/ fan 160°C/gas 4. Tip the chicken mixture into a colander set over a bowl and reserve the liquid. Remove the chicken pieces, pat them dry on kitchen paper and toss in the seasoned flour.

4. Heat the oil and butter in a large, flameproof casserole dish over a medium heat. Add the pancetta and cook for 3–4 minutes. Set aside. Add the chicken and brown on all sides. Set aside.

5. Add the vegetables from the colander and the herbs and mushrooms to the casserole, and cook for 3–4 minutes. Add the extra 1 tablespoon of flour, cook for 1 minute, then stir in the wine. Season, add the chicken and pancetta, and bring to the boil. Cover and cook in the oven for 20 minutes. Garnish with the parsley.

★ DELICIOUS. TIP Use a gutsy red wine such as a Bordeaux for this casserole. The better the wine, the better the dish.

Creamy corn and butter bean chicken

This dish can be made in advance, so freeze it and enjoy it later when there's no time for preparation, just time to cook it.

SERVES 4

TAKES 30 MINUTES

1 tbsp olive oil

4 free-range chicken breasts, skin on

6 rashers rindless streaky bacon, chopped

50g butter

1 onion, finely chopped

2 garlic cloves, crushed

1 red pepper, seeded and chopped

1½ tbsp plain flour

200ml semi-skimmed milk

50ml double cream

326g can sweetcorn, drained

400g can butter beans, drained and rinsed

Handful of fresh parsley, chopped

Green beans, to serve

1. Preheat the oven to 200°C/fan 180°C/gas 6. Heat the oil in a frying pan over a medium–high heat. Add the chicken breasts, skin-side down, and cook for 3–4 minutes until golden. Turn and cook for a further 2 minutes. Remove, add the bacon and fry until golden. Set aside.

2. Wipe the pan with kitchen paper. Melt the butter in the pan, add the onion and garlic, and cook over a gentle heat for 2–3 minutes, until softened. Add the red pepper and cook for 2–3 minutes, until softened.

3. Stir in the flour and cook for 1 minute, then gradually add the milk and stir well until smooth. Stir in the cream. Add the bacon, sweetcorn, butter beans and parsley. Season. Spoon into a 1.5–2 litre ovenproof dish and sit the chicken on top.

4. Bake for 25 minutes, until the chicken is cooked through. Serve with green beans.

★ DELICIOUS. TIP If you wish to freeze this dish, make sure your dish is freezerproof as well as ovenproof.

Spanish chicken and potato stew

It's the spicy paprika-laced sausage that gives this stew its distinctive flavour and rich colour.

SERVES 4

TAKES 45 MINUTES

2 tbsp olive oil

8 free-range chicken pieces (a mixture of thighs and drumsticks)

1 onion, chopped

2 garlic cloves, crushed

110g chorizo, cut into small dice

100ml white wine

2 x 400g cans chopped tomatoes

Few fresh thyme sprigs, plus extra leaves to garnish

2 bay leaves

100ml fresh chicken stock

Good pinch of sugar

650g potatoes, cut into rough chunks

Handful of black olives (optional)

1. Heat the oil in a large saucepan over a medium heat, add the chicken, in batches if necessary, and brown all over. Set aside. Add the onion and garlic to the pan, and cook for 3–4 minutes, stirring frequently, until softened and lightly browned.

2. Add the chorizo and cook for 3–4 minutes, stirring occasionally. Add the wine and reduce by half. Stir in the tomatoes, thyme, bay leaves, stock and sugar. Return the chicken to the pan and push under the sauce. Cover and cook for 20 minutes.

3. Stir in the potatoes and olives, if using, and simmer for a further 35 minutes or until the chicken and potatoes are cooked through. Garnish with the thyme leaves to serve.

★ DELICIOUS. TIP Buy whole, thin chorizo sausages, which are specifically used for cooking in recipes like this.

Fragrant chicken stew

The saffron and fennel in this wonderful stew gives it a mildly exotic flavour.

SERVES 4
TAKES ABOUT 1 HOUR

Good pinch of saffron strands
3 tbsp olive oil
1.5–1.75kg free-range chicken, jointed into 8 pieces (see page 184)
12–16 shallots
2 bulbs fennel, sliced
125g pancetta or bacon lardons
2 garlic cloves, finely chopped
1 tsp fennel seeds, lightly crushed
1 tbsp Pernod (optional)
250ml dry white wine
350ml chicken stock, hot
3 fresh thyme sprigs, leaves picked
2 fresh bay leaves
2 tbsp butter, softened
2 tbsp plain flour
4 tbsp crème fraîche
2 tbsp chopped fresh parsley, to serve

1. Soak the saffron in 1 tablespoon of hot water. Heat the oil in a large, flameproof casserole dish. Season the chicken pieces, add to the oil and brown. Set aside. Add the shallots and fry until golden. Set aside. Add the fennel and fry until golden. Set aside.

2. Pour away all but 1 teaspoon of oil from the casserole, add the pancetta and fry until golden. Add the garlic and fennel seeds, and fry for a few seconds. Add the Pernod, if using, and wine, bubble briefly, then add the stock, herbs and saffron water.

3. Return the chicken and shallots to the casserole, cover and simmer for 5 minutes. Stir in the fennel, cover and simmer for 35 minutes, or until the chicken is tender.

4. Mix the butter and flour together into a smooth paste. Stir in, a little at a time, until the sauce has thickened. Simmer for 2–3 minutes. Stir in the crème fraîche and season. Scatter with the parsley and serve.

Variation For a more down-to-earth version of this stew, replace the saffron and fennel with celery and carrots.

Normandy chicken

Cider and apples are a classic combination in this part of France, and they work incredibly well together in this rich and warming stew.

SERVES 4
READY IN 35 MINUTES

75g butter

8 skinless free-range chicken thighs

6 shallots, halved

4 celery sticks, chopped

300ml apple juice

300ml good-quality fresh chicken stock, hot

200ml crème fraîche

4 eating apples, such as Cox's or Braeburn, cored and cut into wedges

3 tbsp snipped fresh chives, to garnish

French beans or broccoli and mashed potatoes, to serve

1. Heat 50g of the butter in a roasting tin on the hob and brown the chicken thighs all over, turning as needed. Add the shallots and celery, and cook for a few minutes. Pour over the apple juice and stock, and season to taste. Bring to the boil, then cover tightly with foil and cook for 20 minutes, or until the juices run clear when the chicken is pierced. Stir in the crème fraîche and bring just to the boil, then simmer for 1 minute.

2. Heat the rest of the butter in a large frying pan over a medium heat. Add the apple wedges and fry for 5 minutes until lightly browned. Stir the apples into the chicken. Sprinkle with some chopped chives and serve. This is great with French beans or broccoli and mashed potatoes.

★ DELICIOUS. TIP Cooking this in a roasting tin helps save time when browning the chicken, because you can do it all at once rather than in batches.

Variation For a slightly more authentic, adult version of this dish, replace the apple juice with dry cider.

Chicken stew with parsnips, sage and cream

This gloriously creamy stew would make a wonderful winter alternative to the more usual roast.

SERVES 4
READY IN 1¼ HOURS

1 tbsp sunflower oil

1.5kg free-range chicken, jointed into 8 pieces (see page 184)

225g shallots or baby onions, peeled and halved if large

250g small leeks, washed and thickly sliced

450g parsnips, peeled and cut into chunky pieces

300g carrots, peeled and cut into chunky pieces

10 fresh sage leaves, plus 1 tbsp finely chopped fresh sage

3 large fresh thyme sprigs, leaves picked

3 fresh bay leaves

600ml fresh chicken stock

1 tbsp butter, softened

1 tbsp plain flour

4 tbsp double cream

1. Heat the oil in a large, flameproof casserole. Season the chicken pieces, and fry in batches over a medium–high heat until browned. Set aside.

2. Add the shallots or onions to the casserole and fry until browned. Return the chicken to the casserole and scatter with the vegetables and herbs (except the finely chopped sage). Pour over the stock and season. Cover and simmer gently for 30 minutes.

3. Uncover the casserole, remove the chicken and vegetables with a slotted spoon, and set aside. Increase the heat and cook for 10 minutes until the liquid has reduced slightly.

4. Mix the butter and flour together into a paste. Reduce the heat slightly, add the paste and simmer for 2–3 minutes until the sauce has thickened. Stir in the cream and chopped sage, and season to taste. Return the chicken and vegetables to the casserole and reheat briefly.

★ DELICIOUS. TIP Serve with Swiss chard, steamed and tossed with butter and seasoning, and some buttery mashed potatoes.

Spanish cocido

This is the national lunchtime dish of Spain, which has many variations but always contains chickpeas, chicken and pork. It provides you with both starter and main course.

SERVES 6

TAKES 30 MINUTES, 4–6 HOURS COOKING, PLUS OVERNIGHT SOAKING OF CHICKPEAS

Large pinch of saffron

500g packet dried chickpeas, soaked overnight in water

1.5kg whole free-range chicken, cut into 8–12 pieces

300g chorizo sausage, skinned and cut into big chunks

4 pork belly chops, cut into chunks

6 garlic cloves, peeled

6 fresh rosemary sprigs

250g tiny pasta shapes for soup

1 small bunch of flatleaf parsley, finely chopped

Small block of mature Manchego or Parmesan, for grating

1. Put the saffron into a measuring jug and add 1 litre of boiling water. Leave to soak for 10 minutes.

2. Drain the chickpeas and place in a large casserole dish with the chicken, chorizo, pork, garlic and rosemary sprigs. Season generously with salt and pepper then pour over the saffron water, and add another 2 litres of water or until the mixture is fully covered. Cover tightly and place in a cold oven.

3. Turn the oven on to 180°C/fan 160°C/gas 4 and cook for 4–6 hours until the chickpeas and meat are very tender.

4. When ready to serve, put on a pan of salted water for the pasta. Cook for 8 minutes or so, according to the packet instructions, then divide among large, warmed serving bowls. Sprinkle over the parsley and add a good ladleful of the saffron stock, spooned off the top of the cocido, to each bowl. Grate over some Manchego or Parmesan and serve.

5. Once the soup has been eaten, put the rest of the cocido on the table so guests can serve themselves.

★DELICIOUS. TIP Traditionally, cocido is cooked in earthenware pots, but a large casserole dish or large, deep roasting tin, well sealed with foil (you don't want any steam to escape), will also do.

Easy chicken, scrumpy and potato roast

A very simple suppertime dish, all cooked in one roasting tin.

SERVES 4

TAKES 5 MINUTES, PLUS 45 MINUTES IN THE OVEN

1 tbsp olive oil

1.5kg whole free-range chicken, quartered

6 medium white potatoes, quartered

1 tsp dried oregano

330ml scrumpy or cider

1 tbsp cranberry sauce

Steamed green beans, to serve (optional)

1. Preheat the oven to 200°C/fan 180°C/gas 6. Pour the oil into a large roasting tin and place in the oven to heat up for a few minutes. Remove, add the chicken and potatoes to the hot tin, season well and sprinkle over the oregano. Roast for 15 minutes, basting now and then with the hot oil, then remove from the oven and tip away any excess oil.

2. Pour the scrumpy or cider over the chicken and add the cranberry sauce to the tin, stirring it into the juices. Return to the oven for 30 minutes, until the chicken is cooked through and everything is browned. Divide among warmed plates along with any pan juices and serve with steamed green beans, if you like.

★ DELICIOUS. TIP If this becomes a family favourite, you can add 3 eating apples, cored and sliced into wedges, at step 2, to ring the changes.

Creamy chicken, chive and mustard gratin

A really comforting winter dish, with its creamy filling and crunchy, oozy topping.

SERVES 2

TAKES 15 MINUTES, PLUS 20 MINUTES IN THE OVEN

300g floury potatoes, thinly sliced

25g butter

25g plain flour

600ml chicken stock

100ml half-fat crème fraîche

1 tbsp Dijon mustard

Approx. 400g cooked shredded free-range chicken

1 bunch of fresh chives, snipped, plus 2 tbsp extra to garnish

40g Cheshire or Caerphilly cheese, crumbled

40g fresh breadcrumbs

1. Preheat the oven to 200°C/fan 180°C/ gas 6. Bring a saucepan of water to the boil, add the potatoes and cook for 6–8 minutes, until nearly cooked through. Drain well.

2. Make the sauce. Melt the butter in a saucepan, add the flour and cook for 2 minutes, stirring, until it forms a smooth paste. Add the chicken stock, a little at a time, and simmer, stirring all the time, until you have a smooth, thickened sauce.

3. Stir the crème fraîche and mustard into the sauce and heat for a few minutes. Add the chicken and chives, and season to taste.

4. Spoon the mixture into a 1.5-litre gratin or ovenproof baking dish and arrange the potatoes on top. Sprinkle over the cheese and breadcrumbs, and bake for 20 minutes, until the top is pale golden and the filling bubbling hot. Preheat the grill to high, and grill the gratin for 5 minutes to crisp up the topping. Scatter with the extra chives and serve.

Curried chicken and parsnip pie

There's no better way to warm up in the winter months than with a hearty pie topped with a thick crust of crumbly pastry.

SERVES 6
TAKES 1¾ HOURS, 35–40 MINUTES BAKING, PLUS CHILLING

1.5kg whole free-range chicken

2 leeks, washed and sliced

2 bay leaves

225g parsnips, halved lengthways and sliced

1 tbsp sunflower oil

50g butter

1 medium onion, finely chopped

4 garlic cloves, sliced

7.5cm piece fresh root ginger, grated

3 tbsp korma (mild) curry paste

1 tsp ground cumin

¼ tsp cayenne pepper

40g plain flour, plus extra for rolling out

300ml coconut milk

150g cooked green beans, halved

1 bunch of fresh coriander, chopped

500g fresh chilled shortcrust pastry

1 egg, beaten

1. Put the chicken, leeks, bay leaves and ½ teaspoon of salt into a saucepan with 2.25 litres water, bring to the boil and simmer for 45 minutes. Remove the chicken, cool, then break the meat into small, chunky pieces, discarding the skin and bones. Strain the stock into another pan and boil until reduced to 600ml.

2. In another saucepan, fry the parsnips in the oil until golden. Set aside. Melt the butter in the pan, add the onion, garlic and ginger, and cook until soft. Add the curry paste and spices, and cook for 2 minutes. Stir in the flour, then gradually stir in the stock and coconut milk, and continue to stir as you bring it to the boil. Add the parsnips and simmer for 5 minutes.

3. Stir the chicken into the sauce with the beans, coriander and seasoning. Spoon into a deep, 1.75-litre pie dish and push a pie funnel into the centre. Cover and chill for 1 hour.

4. Preheat the oven to 200°C/fan 180°F/gas 6. Roll out the pastry on a lightly floured surface and use it to cover the top of the pie dish. Brush with the beaten egg and bake for 35–40 minutes.

Paprika butter chicken with chickpea couscous

A sumptuous dish with a taste of North Africa.

SERVES 4
READY IN 40 MINUTES

8 skinless free-range chicken thigh fillets

40g butter

2 tbsp runny honey

1 tsp paprika

Juice of 1 lemon, plus wedges to serve

200g couscous

250ml vegetable stock, hot

1 tbsp olive oil

410g can chickpeas, drained and rinsed

Large handful of chopped fresh coriander, plus extra leaves to garnish

1 red chilli, seeded and cut into thin strips, to garnish

Lemon wedges, to serve

1. Preheat the oven to 200°C/fan 180°C/gas 6. Place the chicken in an ovenproof dish and season.

2. Melt the butter in a small saucepan, remove from the heat and stir in the honey, paprika, half the lemon juice and some seasoning. Pour all over the chicken. Bake for 25 minutes, basting with the sauce halfway through cooking, until the chicken is cooked through, golden and sticky.

3. Meanwhile, make the couscous. Put the couscous into a large bowl and pour over the hot stock. Cover the bowl with cling film and set aside for 5 minutes. Fluff up the couscous with a fork, then stir in the remaining lemon juice, olive oil, chickpeas and coriander. Season to taste.

4. Divide the couscous among four warm plates, then put the chicken on top and pour over the sauce. Garnish with the chilli strips and coriander leaves. Serve with the lemon wedges.

oven-baked chicken

Maple-glazed roast chicken

A simple roast chicken with a deliciously sweet and sour flavour.

SERVES 4
TAKES 10 MINUTES, PLUS 1½ HOURS
ROASTING

1.5kg whole free-range chicken
5 tbsp red wine vinegar
4 tbsp maple syrup
1 tsp ground cinnamon
1 tbsp sesame seeds
Roasted carrots and leeks,
  to serve

1. Preheat the oven to 200°C/fan 180°C/gas 6. Season the chicken and pour 2 tablespoons of the red wine vinegar into the body cavity. Put in a roasting tin and roast for 1 hour 10 minutes.

2. Meanwhile, mix together the remaining vinegar with the maple syrup, cinnamon and sesame seeds. Brush half the mixture over the chicken and roast for a further 10 minutes. Brush with the remaining glaze and return to the oven for a final 10 minutes, until the chicken is deeply golden and shiny. Rest for 5 minutes before carving. Serve with roasted carrots and leeks.

Roast chicken with autumn fruits and quinoa

Quinoa (pronounced *keen-wah*) is a nutritious grain from South America; if you can't get it, use rice or bulgur wheat instead.

SERVES 6

TAKES 40 MINUTES, PLUS 1¾ HOURS IN THE OVEN

35g dried cranberries or dried sour cherries

2 tsp chopped fresh thyme leaves, plus 4 extra fresh thyme sprigs

45g butter, softened

2.2kg whole free-range chicken

2 pears, quartered and cored

2 apples, cored and cut into 8 wedges

4 plums, halved and stoned

2 red onions, cut into wedges

2 tbsp light muscovado sugar

2 tbsp olive oil

For the quinoa:

250g quinoa

2 tbsp olive oil

3 garlic cloves, crushed

750ml fresh chicken stock, hot

Extra-virgin olive oil or 20g butter

3 tbsp coarsely chopped fresh flatleaf parsley

1. Soak the cranberries or cherries in boiling water for 10 minutes, then drain. Preheat the oven to 190°C/ fan 170°C/gas 5. Mash the thyme leaves with 30g of the butter and season. Loosen the skin of the chicken and push some of the thyme butter underneath. Put it into a roasting tin, season and roast for 1 hour.

2. Toss the fruit and onions together in a bowl with the thyme sprigs, sugar, olive oil and seasoning. Spoon the mixture around the chicken and coat it in the juices. Dot with the remaining butter, then return to the oven for 45 minutes, turning the fruit once during cooking.

3. When the chicken has 20 minutes left to go, put the quinoa in a sieve and wash well. Heat the olive oil in a saucepan, add the garlic and cook gently until soft. Stir in the quinoa, stock and seasoning and cook for 20 minutes, until soft. Cover for 5 minutes, then fluff up with a fork. Add the olive oil or butter and parsley, and stir through gently. Serve with the roasted chicken and fruit.

Biryani-style baked chicken and rice

This mildly spiced, Indian-inspired supper would go very well with some steamed spinach and mint raita.

SERVES 4

TAKES 20 MINUTES, PLUS 30 MINUTES IN THE OVEN

2 tbsp olive oil

8 bone-in free-range chicken thighs, skin on

1 large onion, finely chopped

3 garlic cloves, sliced

2 tsp garam masala

1 tsp ground ginger

1 green chilli, seeded and finely sliced

300g basmati rice

650ml chicken stock, hot

200g frozen mixed green vegetables

2 tbsp chopped fresh flatleaf parsley, to serve

1. Preheat the oven to 190°C/fan 170°C/ gas 5. Heat the oil in a large roasting tin on the hob. Add the chicken and fry over a high heat until golden brown all over. Remove and set aside.

2. Add the onion and cook gently for 6–8 minutes. Stir in the garlic, garam masala, ginger and chilli. Stir in the rice and cook for 1 minute. Top with the chicken and pour over the stock.

3. Cover tightly with foil and bake for 20 minutes, until the rice has nearly absorbed all of the stock. Add a dash of hot water if the rice looks dry. Uncover and stir in the frozen vegetables. Re-cover and bake for another 8–10 minutes, until everything is cooked. Scatter with parsley to serve.

Variation Use salmon fillets with the skin on instead of the chicken. Pan-fry briefly in step 1, then put on top of the rice in step 3, after the vegetables.

Sticky lime and ginger chicken

A simple but zesty way of jazzing up some chicken thighs.

SERVES 2
TAKES 10 MINUTES, PLUS 20 MINUTES
IN THE OVEN

3 pieces stem ginger in syrup
2 tbsp honey
2 tbsp soy sauce
Finely grated zest of 2 limes
Juice of 1 lime
2 garlic cloves, crushed
6 skinless free-range
  chicken thighs
Steamed basmati rice and
  Tenderstem broccoli, to serve

1. Preheat the oven to 230°C/fan 210°C/gas 8. Drain and finely dice the stem ginger and put it into a large bowl. Add the honey, soy sauce, lime zest, lime juice and garlic, and mix together well.

2. Add the chicken thighs to the bowl and mix so that they become well coated in the glaze. Arrange side by side in a foil-lined or ceramic baking dish and bake for 20 minutes, turning over halfway, until cooked through.

3. Serve with some steamed basmati rice and Tenderstem broccoli.

Caramelised honey, tomato and mustard chicken

Sticky baked chicken cooked in its own barbecue-style sauce.

SERVES 4

TAKES 10 MINUTES, PLUS 35 MINUTES
IN THE OVEN

4 tbsp clear honey

2 tbsp Worcestershire sauce

8 tbsp tomato ketchup

1 tbsp wholegrain mustard

1kg skinless free-range
  chicken drumsticks or thighs,
  or a mixture of both

4 tomatoes, quartered

Potato wedges and salad,
  to serve

1. Preheat the oven to 220°C/fan 200°C/gas 7. In a large roasting tin, mix together the honey, Worcestershire sauce, ketchup and mustard. Season to taste. Add the chicken and toss well until it's evenly coated, then bake for 15 minutes.

2. Turn the chicken pieces over and bake for another 15 minutes.

3. Remove the tin from the oven and spoon off any surface fat from the sauce. Turn the chicken over again, add the tomatoes and stir to coat in the sauce. Bake for a further 5 minutes, until the chicken is cooked, the tomatoes are tender and the sauce is sticky and slightly caramelised. Serve with some potato wedges and salad.

Chicken, soy and honey parcels with spring onion and water chestnut rice

A tasty dish that's high in flavour and low in calories.

SERVES 4

TAKES 15 MINUTES, PLUS 20 MINUTES IN THE OVEN

4 shallots, thinly sliced

4 x 175g skinless free-range chicken breasts

4 tbsp dark soy sauce

4 tsp runny honey

4 tbsp Chinese rice wine or dry sherry

5cm piece fresh root ginger, cut into fine shreds

2 garlic cloves, finely chopped

12 green cardamom pods, cracked

For the spring onion and water chestnut rice:

200g basmati rice

1 bunch of spring onions, trimmed

200g can water chestnuts, drained and chopped

1. Preheat the oven to 180°C/fan 160°C/gas 4. Cut out 4 x 30cm foil squares. Put the shallots and 1 chicken breast on to each square. Bring the sides up slightly around each one and seal at the short ends.

2. Divide the soy sauce, honey and rice wine or sherry, ginger, garlic and cardamom pods among each parcel then fold over and press the edges together well to seal. Put on a baking sheet and bake for 20 minutes or until the chicken is cooked through.

3. Meanwhile, cook the rice according to the packet instructions. Finely shred 2 of the spring onions lengthways and set aside. Thinly slice the rest.

4. Stir the sliced onions and water chestnuts into the cooked rice, and divide among warmed plates. Open up the parcels, lift out the chicken and thickly slice. Place on top of the rice and pour over all the juices from each parcel. Garnish with the shredded spring onions and serve.

Chicken breasts with lemon and tarragon sauce

A simple yet classy dish you could easily serve for a special supper.

SERVES 4
READY IN 55 MINUTES

2 lemons
4 boneless free-range chicken breasts, skin on
8 fresh tarragon sprigs
2 tbsp extra-virgin olive oil
1 tsp sea salt flakes
1 tsp mixed peppercorns, roughly ground
250ml single cream

1. Preheat the oven to 200°C/fan 180°C/gas 6. Cut 7 fine slices from the middle of 1 lemon and juice the remainder of the fruit, along with the other lemon, and set aside. Insert 1 slice of lemon under the skin of each chicken breast along with a sprig of tarragon, then put into a roasting tin. Drizzle with the olive oil and sprinkle over the salt and roughly ground pepper. Roast for 35 minutes.

2. Transfer the chicken to a plate and keep warm. Put the roasting tin over a low heat on the hob and add the lemon juice. Stir with a wooden spatula, scraping up any bits stuck to the bottom of the tin. Add the cream and stir well to heat the mixture through.

3. Return the chicken to the tin and spoon over the sauce. Serve garnished with the remaining tarragon and lemon slices.

★ DELICIOUS. TIP Dauphinoise potatoes go very well with this dish, together with some steamed green vegetables.

Garlic roast chicken and potatoes with rosemary and pancetta

The flavours of the garlic and butter, rosemary and lemon infuse both the chicken and the potatoes cooking beneath.

SERVES 4

TAKES 20 MINUTES, PLUS 1½ HOURS ROASTING

1kg white potatoes, cut into 1cm slices

1 garlic bulb, separated into cloves and peeled

2 fresh rosemary sprigs, leaves only

1 lemon

½ tsp coarse sea salt

Good knob of butter

1.5kg whole free-range chicken

150g pancetta, cubed

300ml white wine

1. Preheat the oven to 200°C/fan 180°C/gas 6. Put the potatoes into a large saucepan of cold water and bring to the boil. Simmer gently for about 5 minutes, until just tender. Drain and set aside.

2. Meanwhile, place the garlic cloves and rosemary leaves into a mini food processor. Peel the zest off the lemon with a potato peeler into the processor, add the sea salt and whiz everything into a paste. Add the butter and some black pepper, and whiz again until well blended.

3. Starting from the neck end, loosen the skin of the chicken with your fingers, and spread the paste under the skin. Quarter the pared lemon and push it into the body cavity.

4. Layer the potatoes and pancetta in a roasting tin, sit the chicken on top and pour over the wine. Season and roast for 1½ hours, until the chicken is golden and cooked through. Rest for 5 minutes, then carve and serve with the potatoes.

Classic roast chicken with chorizo and red onion stuffing

The Mediterranean-style stuffing gives this classic roast chicken a flavour-packed punch.

SERVES 4

TAKES 20 MINUTES, PLUS 1½ HOURS ROASTING

50g piece chorizo, roughly chopped

1 small red onion, finely chopped

40g fresh white breadcrumbs

3 pieces roasted red pepper in oil, drained and chopped

3 tbsp fresh flatleaf parsley, chopped

1 free-range egg yolk

1.5kg whole free-range chicken

1 lemon, quartered

2 tbsp plain flour

150ml red wine

600ml chicken stock, hot

1. Preheat the oven to 200°C/fan 180°C/gas 6. Mix together the chorizo, onion, breadcrumbs, red pepper, parsley, egg yolk and some seasoning. Loosen the skin at the neck end of the chicken and pack in the stuffing, forming a nice rounded shape. Fold the skin back over and secure underneath with a skewer.

2. Push the lemon quarters into the body cavity. Season the chicken, put in a roasting tin and cook for 1½ hours, until golden and cooked through.

3. Lift the chicken on to a board and leave to rest for 5 minutes. Meanwhile, strain the juices and fat from the roasting tin into a jug and allow to settle, then skim off the fat into a bowl. Put the tin back on the hob, add 3 tablespoons of the fat and whisk in the flour. Stir in the wine, bubble rapidly, then add the pan juices and stock, and simmer for 10 minutes until thickened. Carve the chicken and serve with the gravy and some vegetables.

Oriental roast chicken with coconut gravy

A simple blend of oriental spices, lime and herbs flavours the gravy and both the inside and the outside of the bird.

SERVES 4

TAKES 20 MINUTES, PLUS 1½ HOURS ROASTING

1 tbsp vegetable oil
2 tsp Thai spice blend or
  Chinese five spice powder
½ tsp coarse sea salt
Grated zest and juice of 1 lime,
  plus 1 extra lime, halved
1.5kg whole free-range chicken
2 lemongrass stalks, bruised
4 thick slices fresh root ginger
2 fresh or dried lime leaves
200g can coconut cream
200ml chicken stock, hot
1 tbsp Thai red curry paste
Steamed greens and rice,
  to serve

1. Preheat the oven to 200°C/fan 180°C/gas 6. Mix together the oil, spice blend or five spice, salt, lime zest and juice to make a paste. Rub the mixture evenly onto the chicken skin.

2. Pop the lime halves into the body cavity, along with the lemongrass, ginger and lime leaves. Place in a roasting tin and roast for 1½ hours, until the chicken is cooked through. Tip any juices that are inside the body cavity into the tin, then lift the chicken on to a plate and rest for 5 minutes.

3. Meanwhile, pour off the fat from the tin, stir in the coconut cream, stock and curry paste, and cook in the oven for a further 5 minutes, until hot. Carve the chicken and serve with the coconut gravy and some steamed greens, such as pak choi, and rice.

Roasted pesto chicken with polenta and vegetables

A fantastic supper dish packed with some of the best authentic Italian flavours.

SERVES 4

TAKES 15 MINUTES, PLUS 45 MINUTES IN THE OVEN

2 tbsp olive oil
8 free-range chicken thighs
2 tbsp green pesto
500g packet ready-made polenta, cut into cubes
1 large courgette, roughly chopped
150g tomatoes, roughly chopped

1. Preheat the oven to 200°C/fan 180°C/gas 6. Heat the olive oil in a heavy-based frying pan over a high heat. Add the chicken, in batches, and brown on all sides. Remove the pan from the heat and set the chicken aside on a plate.

2. Mix 1 tablespoon of the pesto with the remaining cooking juices in the pan. Arrange the polenta cubes and courgette in a roasting tin. Make spaces in between and add the browned chicken thighs. Drizzle with the pesto pan juices and roast in the oven for 35 minutes.

3. Remove the tin from the oven and scatter with the tomatoes. Return to the oven and roast for a further 10 minutes.

4. Drizzle the chicken and vegetables with the remaining pesto and divide among plates to serve.

Variation Use red pesto for a change instead of green, and then scatter with plenty of fresh basil just before serving.

Roast chicken with bacon, leek and herb stuffing

A classic roast chicken with an old-fashioned, yet very tasty, bacon and herb stuffing.

SERVES 4

TAKES 45 MINUTES, PLUS 1¼ HOURS IN THE OVEN

100g rindless smoked streaky bacon rashers, cut into strips
75g butter, softened
1 medium onion, chopped
100g leek, washed and sliced
90g crustless day-old white bread, cut into 1 cm cubes
1 tsp chopped fresh rosemary, plus extra sprigs
1 tsp chopped fresh thyme, plus extra sprigs
1 tbsp chopped fresh parsley
1 medium egg
4 tbsp milk
1.5kg whole free-range chicken
1 tbsp plain flour
About 450ml chicken stock, hot

1. Preheat the oven to 180°C/fan 160°C/gas 4. Fry the bacon in 15g of the butter until golden. Add the onion and cook until lightly golden. Add the leek and cook for 2–3 minutes. Tip into a bowl. Fry the cubes of bread in another 25g of butter until crisp and golden. Add to the bowl with the herbs and some seasoning, and mix together well. Beat the egg with the milk, stir into the stuffing mixture and leave for 5 minutes.

2. Spoon the stuffing into the chicken's body cavity, push in the extra herbs and seal the opening with a skewer. Truss the chicken, put into a roasting tin and smear with the remaining butter. Season. Roast for 1¼ hours until cooked through.

3. Lift the chicken on to a board and leave to rest. Skim off the excess fat from the pan juices and place over a medium heat. Stir in the flour, then the chicken stock and simmer until slightly thickened. Season. Carve the chicken and serve with the gravy and some vegetables.

Rosemary and honey roast chicken with garlic mash

Honey, rosemary and garlic are a classic combination, or you could vary it with maple syrup and thyme with the lemon.

SERVES 2

TAKES 10 MINUTES, PLUS
20–25 MINUTES IN THE OVEN

2 free-range chicken legs, skin on
2 tbsp runny honey
Juice of 1 small lemon
1 garlic bulb
2 small rosemary sprigs
450g pack fresh potato, carrot and swede mash
Steamed French beans, to serve

1. Preheat the oven to 200°C/fan 180°C/gas 6. Slash the chicken legs a few times on the skin side and place in a roasting tin. Drizzle with the honey and the lemon juice, then season well. Cut the whole bulb of garlic in half horizontally and place in the roasting tin with the chicken.

2. Roast for 15 minutes, then baste and tuck the rosemary sprigs under the chicken. Bake for a further 10 minutes or until the chicken is cooked through and golden, and the pan juices sticky.

3. Meanwhile, heat a 450g pack of fresh potato, carrot and swede mash according to the packet instructions. Squeeze the pulp from the roasted garlic cloves and stir into the mash with some seasoning. Serve mounds of mash on warmed serving plates, top with the roast chicken and drizzle over the sticky pan juices. Delicious served with steamed French beans.

Chicken with asparagus and rice

This is a beautiful dish, both to look at and eat, so save it for a special occasion – if you can.

SERVES 4
READY IN 40–45 MINUTES

225g asparagus spears, woody
  ends snapped off
4 free-range chicken breasts,
  skin on
50ml double cream
2 tbsp olive oil
250g mixed basmati and
  wild rice

For the sauce:
400g can chopped tomatoes
2 tsp roughly chopped fresh
  oregano leaves
3 garlic cloves, roughly chopped
50ml extra-virgin olive oil
100g mascarpone

1. For the sauce, put all the ingredients, except the mascarpone, into a pan and simmer gently for 30 minutes. Blend until smooth, then pass through a sieve into a clean pan. Stir in the mascarpone and season.

2. Meanwhile, cook the asparagus in boiling salted water for 3–4 minutes, until just tender. Drain and set aside. Remove the little fillets from each chicken breast, then cut horizontally into each breast to make a pocket. Season.

3. Put the asparagus into a food processor with the chicken fillets, cream and seasoning. Blend until smooth. Spoon the mixture into each chicken breast pocket and seal the opening with a cocktail stick.

4. Heat the oil in a frying pan over a medium heat. Fry the chicken for 8 minutes on each side until golden and cooked through. Lift on to a board and slice.

5. Meanwhile, cook the rice according to the packet instructions. Warm through the tomato sauce. Spoon the rice on to warmed plates and place the chicken on top. Pour over the sauce and serve.

Chicken and chorizo paella

A tasty and easy supper dish, all cooked in one pan.

SERVES 4
READY IN JUST UNDER 1 HOUR

150g piece chorizo, halved lengthways and sliced

4 large skinless boneless free-range chicken thighs, cut into large chunks

1 tbsp olive oil

1 onion, chopped

2 garlic cloves, crushed

1½ tsp smoked sweet paprika

300g paella or risotto rice

Approx. 1 litre chicken stock, hot

1 red pepper and 1 yellow pepper, seeded and sliced

75g fine green beans, trimmed and blanched

3 large ripe plum tomatoes, cut into chunky pieces

15g fresh flatleaf parsley, leaves picked and chopped

Lemon wedges, to serve

1. Heat a large, deep frying pan over a medium heat. Add the chorizo and cook, stirring occasionally, for 3–4 minutes, until it's golden and the oil has been released. Remove with a slotted spoon and set aside.

2. Add the chicken and cook for 3–4 minutes, stirring until golden. Set aside with the chorizo.

3. Add the olive oil and onion to the pan, and cook, stirring, for 6–8 minutes, until softened. Add the garlic and paprika, and cook for 1 minute. Stir in the rice, then the stock and simmer for 10 minutes, stirring occasionally.

4. Return the chicken to the pan with the peppers, beans and tomatoes. Stir and cook for 5 minutes, adding a little more stock or hot water if it starts to look dry. Season and stir in the chorizo and parsley. Cook for 5 minutes or until the rice is just tender, and the liquid has been absorbed. Serve with lemon wedges.

Red wine chicken with peppers and olives

This dish is perfect for making ahead and freezing; it just needs to be thawed out then re-heated before serving.

SERVES 4
READY IN 1 HOUR

1 large whole free-range chicken, cut into 8 pieces
2 tbsp plain flour, seasoned
2 tbsp sunflower oil
70g pancetta or smoked streaky bacon rashers, cut into cubes
3 garlic cloves, finely sliced
1 red onion, cut into wedges
2 each red and yellow peppers, halved, seeded and sliced into strips
300ml red wine
Leaves of 1 fresh rosemary sprig
Leaves of 1 fresh thyme sprig
100g mixed green and black olives
1 large bunch of flatleaf parsley, finely chopped
Sautéed rosemary potatoes, to serve

1. Put the chicken in a large bowl and toss in the seasoned flour.

2. Heat the oil in a large, flameproof casserole, add the chicken pieces skin-side down in a single layer and cook for 4–5 minutes, until golden. Turn and cook for a further 3–4 minutes. Remove from the pan and set aside.

3. Add the pancetta and cook for 2–3 minutes, until golden. Stir in the garlic, red onion, peppers and any remaining seasoned flour, and cook for 5 minutes. Pour in the wine and simmer rapidly for a few minutes. Turn down the heat and return the chicken and any juices to the pan.

4. Add the rosemary and thyme and some seasoning. Cover and simmer for 30 minutes, until the chicken is cooked and the sauce is reduced. Stir in the olives and parsley, and simmer for a further 2 minutes. Serve with some sautéed rosemary potatoes.

★DELICIOUS. TIP Freeze for up to 3 months. Defrost thoroughly at room temperature, then transfer to a roasting tin or baking dish and cover with foil. Reheat at 180°C/fan 160°C/gas 4 for 30 minutes, until piping hot. Uncover for the final 5 minutes of cooking.

Chicken, tomato and mozzarella gnocchi

This is comfort food at its best: perfect for supper on a cold winter night.

SERVES 4
READY IN 25 MINUTES

1 small broccoli head, cut into small florets
500g pack fresh gnocchi
1 tbsp olive oil
4 skinless free-range chicken breasts
1 small onion, sliced
1 garlic clove, crushed
400g can chopped tomatoes with herbs
150g pack mozzarella, drained and roughly chopped
Green salad, to serve

1. Cook the broccoli in boiling salted water for 2–3 minutes, until just tender. Remove with a slotted spoon, drain on kitchen paper and set aside. Add the gnocchi to the boiling water and cook according to the packet instructions. Drain and set aside.

2. Put a large frying pan over a high heat and add the oil. Season the chicken, add to the pan and cook for 2–3 minutes on each side, until browned. Reduce the heat to Medium, add the onion and garlic, and cook for 5 minutes until softened.

3. Preheat the grill to High. Add the tomatoes to the pan, quarter-fill the can with water and swish out into the pan. Simmer for 5 minutes, until reduced slightly and the chicken is cooked through. Stir in the broccoli and gnocchi, season and heat through.

4. Transfer to a shallow ovenproof dish. Scatter with the mozzarella and grill for 2–3 minutes, until the cheese begins to melt. Serve with a green salad.

Variation For a vegetarian supper, replace the chicken with some Mediterranean vegetables, such as peppers and courgettes, and fry them along with the onion and garlic.

Chicken and broccoli stir-fry with wholewheat spaghetti

A speedy supper dish, requiring minimum effort for maximum taste.

SERVES 2
READY IN 20 MINUTES

75g wholewheat spaghetti
1 tsp sunflower oil
2 skinless boneless free-range chicken breasts, cut into thin strips
200g purple sprouting broccoli spears (or broccoli, cut into small florets)
1 tbsp soy sauce
2 tbsp sweet chilli sauce
100g beansprouts
1 mild red chilli, seeded and finely chopped
4 spring onions, thinly sliced
2 tsp sesame seeds, toasted

1. Cook the spaghetti in boiling salted water according to the packet instructions. Meanwhile, heat the oil in a wok and stir-fry the chicken for 2 minutes, then add the broccoli and stir-fry for a further 2 minutes.

2. Mix together the soy sauce, sweet chilli sauce and 2 tablespoons of water. Add to the pan and, once bubbling, stir in the beansprouts and chilli. Cook for a minute or so until the beansprouts look a little translucent.

3. Drain the spaghetti and add to the pan with the spring onions and sesame seeds. Stir together and serve piping hot.

★ DELICIOUS. TIP Unless you have a super-sized wok, never attempt a stir-fry for more than two people, as a large quantity of ingredients makes it very difficult for the wok to maintain the high heat essential for good results.

Variation For a Japanese twist, use wholewheat soba noodles instead of the spaghetti, and tamari instead of soy sauce.

Lemon and basil grilled chicken with creamy polenta

This refreshing dish is created using classic Italian flavours – basil, lemon and creamy blue cheese.

SERVES 4
READY IN 30 MINUTES

Grated zest of 1 lemon, plus a good squeeze of fresh lemon juice
Large handful of fresh basil leaves
1 small garlic clove
½ tsp coarse sea salt
2 tbsp olive oil
4 skinless free-range chicken breast fillets
300ml milk
150g instant polenta
150g dolcelatte or Gorgonzola, diced
Green beans and lemon wedges, to serve (optional)

1. Preheat the grill to Medium–High. Put the lemon zest, basil, garlic and sea salt into a mini food processor, and whiz until finely chopped. Add the oil and lemon juice, and whiz again to make a loose paste.

2. Rub the paste over the chicken breasts. Lay them side by side in a foil-lined grill pan and cook for 12–15 minutes, turning them over halfway through, until they are golden brown and cooked through.

3. Meanwhile, pour the milk into a large pan with 400ml of water. Add a little salt and bring to the boil. Reduce the heat to low, then add the polenta and beat with a wooden spoon until smooth. Cook, stirring, for 4–5 minutes, until thickened.

4. Stir the cheese into the polenta, then quickly spoon the mixture into 4 shallow bowls. Top each with a chicken breast and serve immediately with green beans and a wedge of lemon, if you like.

★ DELICIOUS. TIP Soft polenta sets fairly quickly, so don't cook it until just before serving. If it does start to set before you're ready to serve, add a splash of hot water from the kettle and beat with a wooden spoon to soften again.

Pan-fried chicken in a cheese and thyme crust

In a crust like this, cooking chicken breasts quickly guarantees they stay juicy and succulent.

SERVES 4
READY IN 20 MINUTES

Pinch of saffron threads
4 skinless boneless free-range chicken breasts
1 tbsp plain flour
1 large egg, beaten
4 tbsp olive oil
8 tbsp finely grated Grana Padano or Parmesan
1 tbsp chopped fresh thyme, plus extra sprigs to garnish
Herby mashed potatoes and lemon wedges, to serve

1. Put the saffron in a bowl, add a tablespoon of boiling water and set aside for a few minutes to soak.

2. Meanwhile, cut each chicken breast in half lengthways to make 8 thin pieces, then dust them very lightly with the flour.

3. Crack the egg into the bowl of saffron water. Add a good grinding of black pepper and beat well.

4. Heat half the oil in a large, non-stick frying pan over a medium heat. Mix the cheese and thyme together on a plate. Dip half the chicken first in the egg mixture, then coat in the cheese mixture. Fry for 5 minutes on each side until crisp, golden and cooked through. Don't be tempted to lift or turn the chicken too soon whilst cooking, or the crust might stick to the bottom of the pan. Remove and keep warm while you cook the remaining chicken. Garnish with the thyme sprigs and serve with herby mashed potatoes and lemon wedges.

★ DELICIOUS. TIP These cheese-and thyme-coated chicken strips are also fantastic served inside some crusty bread, together with some garlic mayonnaise and salad.

Chicken scallopini

Using a tub of ready-made tomato pasta sauce means this meal can be on the table in less than half an hour.

SERVES 4
READY IN 25 MINUTES

4 skinless free-range chicken breasts
Olive oil, for brushing
500g tub fresh tomato pasta sauce
75g pitted black olives
Handful of shredded fresh basil leaves, plus 8 whole leaves
125g mozzarella ball, cut into 8 thin slices and patted dry with kitchen paper
4 slices Parma ham
Olive-oil mashed potatoes and green vegetables, to serve

1. Using a rolling pin, flatten the chicken breasts between 2 sheets of cling film into 5mm-thick escalopes. Brush with a little olive oil, season, and cook, one or two at a time, in a hot frying pan for 3–4 minutes, turning halfway, until cooked and golden.

2. Meanwhile, preheat the grill to High. In a small pan, heat the pasta sauce until hot. Stir in the olives and shredded basil.

3. Pour the sauce into a large, shallow ovenproof dish and lay the chicken side by side on top. Cover each escalope with 2 mozzarella slices, 2 basil leaves and 1 slice of Parma ham. Grill for 5–6 minutes, until bubbling. Serve with olive-oil mash and green vegetables.

Chicken and cashew nut stir-fry

This dish is utterly delicious and unbelievably simple – quick to prepare and quick to cook.

SERVES 4
READY IN 30 MINUTES

1 tbsp groundnut oil
450g skinless free-range chicken breasts, diced
200g dried medium egg noodles
1 large carrot, quartered and cut into matchsticks
2 celery sticks, finely sliced
1 red pepper, seeded and sliced
1 mild red chilli, seeded and sliced
Thumb-sized piece fresh root ginger, grated
1 large garlic clove, finely chopped
2 pak choi, stems sliced and leaves torn
1 bunch of spring onions, trimmed and sliced
300g beansprouts
100g cashew nuts, toasted

For the sauce:
1 tbsp cornflour
3 tbsp soy sauce
3 tbsp Chinese rice wine or dry sherry
1 tbsp toasted sesame oil

1. Bring a pan of water to the boil. Meanwhile, mix all the ingredients for the sauce together in a small bowl, season with black pepper and set aside.

2. Put the wok over a high heat for 1 minute. Add the groundnut oil and chicken, and stir-fry for 4–5 minutes until nearly cooked. Remove with a slotted spoon and set aside.

3. Drop the noodles into the pan of boiling water and cook according to the packet instructions. Add the carrot, celery, pepper and chilli to the wok, and stir-fry for 3–4 minutes. Add the ginger, garlic and pak choi stems to the wok, and stir-fry for 2–3 minutes. Add the onions and beansprouts, and stir-fry for 2 minutes.

4. Return the chicken to the wok, along with the pak choi leaves. Stir-fry for 1 minute. Add the sauce and stir-fry for 1–2 minutes, until the sauce has thickened. Drain the noodles. Stir in the cashews and serve with the cooked noodles.

Yakitori chicken

Yakitori, the classic Japanese glaze, gives this chicken dish a beautiful glossy, mahogany appearance.

SERVES 4

TAKES 15 MINUTES, PLUS 15 MINUTES MARINATING

3 large skinless boneless free-range chicken breasts, cut into thin strips
6 tbsp dark soy sauce
4 tbsp clear honey
2 tbsp dry sherry
1 tbsp sesame oil
450g pack crunchy stir-fry vegetables (with pak choi, water chestnuts, beansprouts, carrots, peppers, red onions and herbs, etc.)
1 tbsp cornflour
Flat rice noodles, to serve

1. Mix the chicken, soy sauce, honey and sherry together in a shallow, non-metallic dish. Cover and set aside to marinate for 15 minutes.

2. Heat the oil in a large wok or frying pan over a high heat. Remove the chicken from the marinade with a slotted spoon, add to the wok and stir-fry for 5 minutes, until cooked through.

3. Remove the herbs from the pack of stir-fry vegetables and set aside in cold water. Tip the vegetables into the pan and stir-fry for 1 minute.

4. Mix any remaining marinade with the cornflour until well combined and pour into the pan. Stir-fry for 1–2 minutes until everything is cooked and coated in the sauce. Serve spooned over some cooked flat rice noodles and scatter with the reserved herbs.

Pan-fried chicken on chilli rocket with charmoula butter

Charmoula is a fresh spice paste from North Africa, which gives this chicken a fantastically exotic flavour.

SERVES 4
READY IN 30 MINUTES

2 red chillies, seeded
175g butter, softened
Small handful of chopped fresh coriander
2 garlic cloves, crushed
1 tsp ground cumin
Good pinch of saffron strands
Grated zest of 1 lemon
4 free-range chicken breasts, skin on
4 tbsp olive oil, plus a little for brushing
1 tbsp balsamic vinegar
1 large bag wild rocket

1. Finely chop 1 chilli and put it into a bowl with the softened butter, coriander, garlic, cumin, saffron and lemon zest, and mix together well. Spoon on to a sheet of greaseproof paper, roll up into a 2.5cm-wide log, then twist each end of the paper like a Christmas cracker. Chill until required.

2. Heat a griddle pan until hot. Brush the chicken with a little oil and season well. Sear skin-side down for 5–6 minutes, turn over and cook for a further 6–8 minutes until cooked through.

3. Just before the chicken is ready, thinly slice the remaining chilli and put it into a large bowl. Whisk in the olive oil, balsamic vinegar and some seasoning. Add the rocket and toss together well.

4. Divide the dressed rocket among four plates and top each with a chicken breast. Slice the butter and put 2 slices on top of each chicken breast. Serve as soon as the butter begins to melt on to the chicken.

★ DELICIOUS. TIP Try cooking this chicken on the barbecue too, since the slightly smoky flavour goes particularly well with the charmoula butter.

Southern-fried chicken with cream gravy and sweetcorn mash

A comforting supper dish inspired by the flavours of the southern states of North America.

SERVES 2
READY IN 20 MINUTES

300g potatoes
15g butter, plus extra for the mash
198g can sweetcorn, drained
2 tbsp plain flour
1 tsp chilli powder
2 skinless boneless free-range chicken breasts
Splash of white wine
142ml carton double cream
Fresh flatleaf parsley leaves, to garnish

1. Cut the potatoes into even-sized pieces and cook in boiling salted water for 12 minutes, or until tender. Drain and mash with a knob of butter until smooth. Stir in the sweetcorn and some seasoning, cover and keep warm.

2. Meanwhile, combine the flour and chilli powder. Toss the chicken in the chilli flour, shaking off any excess. Melt the 15g of butter in a frying pan and cook the chicken over a medium heat for 5–6 minutes on each side, until golden and tender (be careful not to let the butter burn).

3. Push the chicken to one side. Add the wine to the pan and leave to bubble for 1 minute. Add the cream, bring to the boil and simmer until slightly thickened. Season well. Spoon the sweetcorn mash onto warmed plates, add the chicken and pour over the sauce. Scatter with parsley and serve.

★DELICIOUS. TIP Try adding a touch of wine and cream to your gravy next time you make a roast chicken.

Griddled chicken with spiced tomato couscous

This dish goes particularly well with some cool and refreshing garlic and cucumber tzatziki.

SERVES 2
READY IN 12 MINUTES

2 free-range chicken breasts, skin on
1 tbsp mild curry paste
Juice of ½ lime
150g couscous
Good handful of cherry tomatoes
Small handful of fresh mint leaves, to garnish

1. Heat a griddle pan until hot, add the chicken breasts, skin-side down, and cook for 10–12 minutes, turning once halfway through.

2. Meanwhile, measure out 200ml of boiling water and stir in the curry paste and the lime juice. Put the couscous into a bowl, pour over the liquid, cover, and set aside for 5 minutes.

3. Quarter the cherry tomatoes and mix them into the couscous. Divide the couscous between 2 plates, place a chicken breast on top and garnish with the mint leaves.

Chicken sauté with white wine, shallots and tarragon

Be sure to use homemade chicken stock in this recipe, rather than from a cube, or your sauce will be far too salty.

SERVES 4
READY IN ABOUT 1 HOUR

600ml homemade chicken stock

3 tbsp olive oil

1 whole free-range chicken, about 1.75kg, jointed into 8 pieces (see page 184) and skin removed

12 small shallots, peeled

8 small garlic cloves

600ml medium–dry white wine

2 tbsp chopped fresh tarragon leaves, plus 8 small sprigs to garnish

4 fresh bay leaves

1 heaped tbsp half-fat crème fraîche

1. Put the chicken stock into a pan and boil until reduced by half – to about 300ml.

2. Meanwhile, heat 2 tablespoons of the oil in a non-stick frying pan over a medium–high heat. Add the chicken and fry for 5–8 minutes, until richly golden on all sides. Set aside.

3. Wipe the pan clean, return to the heat and add the remaining oil. Add the shallots and garlic, and fry until lightly browned. Set aside with the chicken.

4. Add the wine to the pan and boil for 10 minutes, until reduced by three-quarters. Stir in the chicken stock, tarragon and bay leaves. Return the chicken to the pan with the shallots and garlic. Cover and simmer for 20 minutes. Turn the chicken and cook, uncovered, for 25 minutes, until the sauce is nicely reduced.

5. Lift the chicken on to a serving platter and scatter over the shallots and garlic. Stir the crème fraîche into the simmering sauce, season, and pour over the chicken. Scatter with tarragon sprigs and serve.

★ DELICIOUS. TIP Boiling down the wine cooks off the calorific alcohol and gives the sauce a lovely savoury flavour.

Chicken, broad bean and chorizo rice

Look out for Spanish short grain rice called Calasparra for this dish; the grains remain beautifully separate during cooking.

SERVES 4
READY IN 1 HOUR

2 tbsp olive oil
6 boneless skinless free-range chicken thighs, halved
100g chorizo, diced
2 medium onions, chopped
3 garlic cloves, chopped
1 green pepper, seeded and sliced
200g paella rice
Pinch of saffron (optional)
100ml white wine
500ml hot chicken stock or water
400g broad beans, blanched and peeled, if you prefer

1. Heat the oil in a wide-bottomed pan and brown the chicken pieces all over. Remove and set aside.

2. Add the chorizo and fry for about 1 minute. Stir in the onions, garlic, pepper and some seasoning. Cover, lower the heat and 'sweat' for about 10–15 minutes, stirring occasionally.

3. Return the chicken to the pan. Add the rice, saffron (if using) and wine. Stir and turn up the heat. Let the wine bubble fiercely for 2–3 minutes, add the stock and reduce the heat. Cover and cook for 15 minutes, then add the beans and cook for 5 minutes – the rice should be tender but with bite. Stir once, rest for 5 minutes, then serve.

★ DELICIOUS. TIP Garnish this with a good handful of chopped fresh parsley or coriander leaves.

Tips for buying poultry

Quite simply, good poultry that is worth eating is the result of good breeding, welfare, and its age at slaughter. Here are a few pointers for what you should look for when buying poultry:

● If a chicken is labelled as an individual breed or is attributed to a particular farm, this usually denotes a good-quality bird. Only small producers rear specific, slow-maturing breeds, and they usually practise good husbandry.

● If a bird has a long, lean body, it's often a sign that it has been allowed to run around freely, outdoors. The breasts will seem less plump, but their flavour will more than compensate for this.

● The skin of a chicken should be quite dry to the touch. A bird that has been dry-plucked will give the cooked skin a crisper finish.

● The meat should be firm and moist, but not wet. It should also have an attractive, deep-pink colour, and smell fresh and appetising.

Ethical eating

There's a lot of encouragement to eat 'ethical' chicken, but what does this mean, exactly? Go to a chiller cabinet in any supermarket, and you'll be faced with an array of descriptive words on chicken packaging, but some phrases can give a misleading impression of the conditions in which a bird has been kept. Here's a guide to help avoid confusion:

FREE-RANGE
To qualify for use of this term, chickens need only to be kept in conditions sometimes just marginally better than those for the average battery chicken. Yes, they are less cramped and have access to the outside, but in reality the birds are so stressed and confused that it only makes a small amount of difference to their lives. The birds often come from the breed commonly used as battery chickens, too, which means they will put on weight quickly and easily, especially over the breast.

TRADITIONAL FREE-RANGE

There is a small improvement here. These birds are housed in mobile homes that can be wheeled to fresh pastures and are less densely packed. There is more outdoor space available per bird. They also have a minimum slaughter age of 81 days, rather than the more commercial age of 41–43 days; because they are allowed more time to mature, the farmers can afford to use slower-growing breeds that are renowned for having a better flavour and texture.

ORGANIC FREE-RANGE

These birds have been allowed to mature naturally, and have been reared for 80–90 days, rather than 41–43 days. They come from small flocks that have been allowed to roam freely outdoors, foraging for insects and scraps as well as being fed on organic feed, grain and fresh water. The best come directly from small producers.

FREE-RANGE TOTAL FREEDOM

These birds are reared in open-air runs of unlimited size, so they have much more space available to them, and they must have continual access to the outside during daylight hours. They are left to mature for 60–80 days.

CORN-FED

Although the label might lead us to think that these birds have led a better life, having been fed on grain rather than artificial feed, this is sadly not always the case. Many are still intensively reared.

POULET DE BRESSE

This is the Rolls Royce of chickens: it is a unique breed from France, which is reared under very strict regulations and even carries its own 'Appellation Contrôlée' – as good wines do. It has a superb flavour, due to its grain-rich diet and careful rearing, and it is also left to hang for a short time, much like a game bird, before being sold. These birds are available from specialist butchers.

How to joint a chicken into 8 pieces

To joint a whole bird easily and successfully, it is imperative to use a very sharp knife, and have a sharp, strong pair of scissors or some poultry shears to hand.

• First, there is a special little piece of meat, called the 'oyster', that you can rescue from the stockpot. Turn the chicken over so that the breast is underneath. Take a small, sharp knife and, where the thigh joint joins the backbone, cut part-way around the small nodule of flesh lying in its own bony dip.

• Now turn the bird back over and ease the legs gently away from the body. Cut through the skin between the thigh and the body, as far around the leg as possible, keeping the knife as close to the body as you can. (A)

• Pull the leg away from the body more vigorously and bend it back on itself so that you expose the thigh joint and the ball breaks free of the socket. Cut between the ball and socket to release the leg, and cut through any flesh still attached to the carcass. The 'oyster' should still be attached to the thigh. (B)

• Place the legs, skin-side up on a board and cut off the knuckle joint at the end of the drumstick. Feel and bend the joint joining the thigh to the drumstick to locate the gap in the bone. Cut through this to separate the leg into two. Repeat with the other leg.

• Now take the breast and wing off the carcass in one piece. To do this, make a cut through the skin and flesh running along either side of the cartilaginous ridge of the breast bone. Cut the breast meat away from the bones, working from the body-cavity end of the chicken down towards and under the wing joint, keeping the knife as close to the carcass as possible. Finish by cutting through the joint where the wing is attached, giving you a breast with its wing attached. Repeat with the other breast and wing.

• Lay each of the breast-wing pieces skin-side up the board and cut slightly on the diagonal into two, leaving about one-third of the breast meat attached to the wing. Cut off the almost meatless tips of the wings, if you wish.

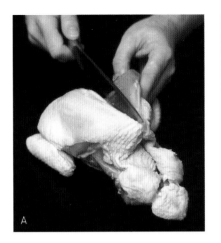

FINAL

Poached chicken broth

This recipe will give you about 2.5 litres of beautifully flavoured chicken stock, and provide you with about 1kg of cooked chicken meat with which to make the recipes on page 14 (Spiced chicken noodle soup), page 116 (Creamy chicken, chive and mustard gratin) and page 24 (Herby chicken and lemon rice). Any extra can be frozen for later use. Cover the chicken meat with the stock before freezing and strain the meat from the stock before using, This will help to keep it moist.

TAKES 1½ HOURS
MAKES ABOUT 2.5 LITRES

1 large (about 2.5kg) good-quality free-range chicken, without giblets
10 peppercorns
4 bay leaves
2 washed leeks or onions, roughly chopped
4 thin carrots, halved lengthways
3 celery sticks, halved
1 small bunch fresh thyme
1 small bunch fresh parsley
2 tsp celery salt

1. Wash the chicken well and place in a large saucepan or flameproof casserole with the peppercorns, bay leaves, leeks or onions, carrots and celery. Tie up the herbs with string and add to the pan with the celery salt. Pour over 4 litres of cold water to cover the chicken and place on the hob. Cover and bring to the boil. Reduce the heat and simmer for 1 hour, until the chicken is cooked through. Leave in the broth until cool enough to handle.

2. Remove the chicken from the broth and place on a board to cool completely. Remove the cooled meat from the chicken carcass and slice or shred. To freeze, divide the meat among 2 or 3 plastic containers with lids and pour over the broth. Cover, label and freeze. Defrost at room temperature (it will take about 6–8 hours) before using.

Quick chicken stock

This classic recipe for chicken stock will make good use of the leftovers from a roast and makes about 1.75 litres. Lots of recipes call for stock, and you can either use it fresh once made, or freeze it. You could even freeze it in ice-cube trays so that you can add a few cubes on those occasions when you only need a little stock to add a bit of flavour to a dish.

TAKES 1¼ HOURS
MAKES ABOUT 1.75 LITRES

Bones from 1.5kg uncooked free-range chicken or 500g chicken wings or drumsticks
1 large carrot, chopped
2 celery sticks, sliced
2 leeks, washed and sliced
2 bay leaves
2 large fresh thyme sprigs
4 peppercorns

1. Put all the ingredients together in a large pan, pour over 2.25 litres of cold water and place on the hob. Bring to the boil, skimming off any scum from the surface as it appears. Leave to simmer very gently for 1 hour. It is important not to let it boil.

2. Strain the stock through a sieve into a bowl and use as required, or cover and leave to cool, chill or freeze for later use.

Index

Picture and recipe credits

Harper Collins and delicious. would like to thank the following for providing photographs:

Steve Baxter p13, p17, p21, p61, p75, p77, p83, p91, p119, p131, p147, p149; Peter Cassidy p15, p25, p27, p31, p85, p87, p89, p103, p105, p117, p155; Jean Cazals p65; Ewen Francis p95, p137; Jonathan Gregson p33, p35, p45, p165; Janine Hosegood p37; Mark Hudson p49, p51; Richard Jung p127, p135, p163; Emma Lee p69; Gareth Morgans p167, p175; Lis Parsons p19, p39, p47, p53, p59, p93, p109, p121, p133, p145, p161; Michael Paul p29, p55, p107, p111; Craig Robertson p23, p73, p113,

p115, p129, p153, p157; Deidre Rooney p177; Brett Stevens p71; Clive Streeter p57; Lucinda Symons p63; Peter Thiedeke p101; Philip Webb p99, p125, p139, p141, p143; Stuart West p43, p79, p81; Kate Whitaker p179; Rob White p181

With thanks, too, for the following for creating the recipes for delicious. used in this book:

Felicity Barnum Bobb p108; Kate Belcher p38, p42, p48, p56, p132, p154, p158, p166, p168; Katie Bishop p70; Angela Boggiano p14, p24, p78, p80, p116, p156; Angela Boggiano and Kate Belcher p22; Angela Boggiano and Alice Hart

p128; Lorna Brash p28, p58, p170; Sally Clarke p46; Matthew Drennan p20, p30, p36, p60, p64, p90, p92, p102, p104, p120, p172, p174, p176; Silvana Franco p98, p112, p114, p124, p138, p140, p142, p160, p162, p164; Brian Glover p54; Angela Hartnett p62; Diana Henry p126; Catherine Hill p44, p50, p74, p76, p100, p148; Debbie Major p26, p52, p68, p82, p88, p106, p110, p118, p134, p146, p178; Kim Morphew p144; Tom Norrington-Davies p16, p32, p34, p180; Meena Pathak and Sunil Menon p84, p86; Simon Rimmer p152; Linda Tubby p94, p136; Jenny White p12, p72; Mitzie Wilson p18